BY THE AUTHOR

Novels
Surviving Sting
Kiss Me Softly, Amy Turtle
Do I Love You?

Poetry
The Right Suggestion
Catch a Falling Tortoise
An Artist Goes Bananas

Criticism
Fiction from the Furnace
Student Guide to Philip Roth
Laughing at the Darkness
Reading *Catch-22*
Reading Toni Morrison's *Beloved*
Storytelling: Narratology for Critics and Creative Writers
Philip Roth Through the Lens of Kepesh
(with Samantha Roden)
The Enigmas of Confinement: A History and Poetics of Flash Fiction
Lydia Davis: A Study

Philosophy
The Philosophy of Humour

As Editor
Loffing Matters
The Tipping Point

ALLEN GINSBERG

ALLEN GINSBERG
Cosmopolitan Comic

PAUL McDONALD

Greenwich Exchange
London

Acknowledgements

Some of the ideas that feature in this book were first presented in a paper delivered at the Fourth European Beat Studies Network Conference, Université Libre de Bruxelles, 2015. I would like to thank my fellow EBSN members for their valuable feedback, not least the consistently inspirational Dr Franca Bellarsi.

Greenwich Exchange, London

First published in Great Britain in 2020
All rights reserved

Paul McDonald © 2020

This book is sold subject to the conditions that it shall not, by way of trade or otherwise, be lent, resold, hired out or otherwise circulated without the publisher's prior consent in any form of binding or cover other than that in which it is published and without a similar condition including this condition being imposed on the subsequent purchaser.

Printed and bound by imprintdigital.com
Cover design by December Publications
Tel: 07951511275

Greenwich Exchange Website: www.greenex.co.uk

Cataloguing in Publication Data is available from the British Library

Cover art: Allen Ginsberg
(reproduced courtesy of Wikimedia Commons)

ISBN: 978-1-910996-39-3

CONTENTS

Introduction *11*

Early Work and Influences *12*

Ginsberg's Blake Vision *17*

The Cultural Moment of 'Howl' *18*

'Howl' and Spontaneity *20*

'Howl' and Autobiography *22*

'Howl' Part II: Moloch *23*

'Howl' Part III: Rockland *25*

Footnote: The Spiritual 'Howl' *27*

'Howl', Madness, and the Id *28*

'Howl' and Humour *28*

Other Poems of the Late 1950s *30*

'Supermarket in California' *30*

'Sunflower Sutra' *32*

'America' *35*

'Death to Van Gogh's Ear!' *38*

Ginsberg the Confessional Poet *41*

'Kaddish' *43*

'Kaddish' Part I *44*

'Kaddish' Part II *45*

'Kaddish' Parts III, IV and V *48*

Buddhism *49*

'Angkor Wat' and *Planet News* 51

Change: *Kyoto-Tokyo Express* 53

'Wichita Vortex Sutra' 55

Ginsberg and L=A=N=G=U=A=G=E 58

Mantras and Chanting 59

Chanting and Carnival: 'Thoughts on Sitting Breathing' 61

'Mugging' 63

Cosmopolitan Comedy: Zen and Humour 65

Ginsberg the Zen Trickster 69

Carnival Again: 'Sphincter' 73

Dissenting Voices: Ginsberg's Detractors 76

Conclusion 80

Selected Bibliography 84

Introduction

Allen Ginsberg was among the best-known poets of the twentieth century, and his work continues to resonate decades after his death in 1997. As cultural icon, his life has been much discussed: there are several major biographies and countless books about Ginsberg as a founder member of the Beat Generation in the 1950s. But the poetry itself hasn't always attracted the scholarly attention it deserves, despite Ginsberg's acknowledged status as an innovator. There have been surprisingly few critical studies, and the scholarship that exists often focuses on 'Howl', the controversial piece that brought him to the attention of the world in 1956. This study reassesses his writing from a modern perspective, offering a succinct and accessible reading of his oeuvre, including some of the unjustly neglected late poems. It takes existing criticism as a starting point, but presents an original reading that, among other things, emphasises the importance of humour in Ginsberg's work. A profound comic sensibility pervades his aesthetic, both in terms of his language and his various personas as Holy Fool, Schlemiel, and Trickster; I argue that this aspect of his work is one of its most enduring and important features, and one of its delights.

Early Work and Influences

Born in New Jersey in 1926, Ginsberg took his search for form and voice very seriously as a young man, experimenting with various approaches to writing. It's often said that much of his early work was marred by the use of conventional poetic structures which didn't suit him. This partly reflects the influence of his father, Louis Ginsberg (1895-1976), who was himself a poet drawn to traditional metrical verse forms. In his youth Ginsberg is extremely conscious of, and constrained by, his father's aesthetic, but he became increasingly aware that Louis's lyric style was wrong for him, and signs of conflict in his early work reveal how he struggled with such traditions. Bill Morgan, for instance, describes one piece of juvenilia, 'The Last Voyage', which exhibits a tension of sorts between Ginsberg's penchant for rebellion, on the one hand, and conformity on the other. While the poem is modelled on Rimbaud's *Le Bateau Ivre* and Baudelaire's *Le Voyage*, it is cast in 'iambic quatrains somewhat imitative of his father's poetries'[1]. In other words, while it references two writers who are representative of literary experiment and subversion, its adherence to his father's style implies a reliance on tradition and filial influence. Ultimately Ginsberg didn't see Louis as a competent literary father, and there followed rather self-conscious attempts on Ginsberg's part to distance himself from Louis. James Breslin, for instance, shows how Ginsberg deemed his father's work inferior to his own, and felt compelled to say so: when in later life he penned an introduction to a volume of his father's verse, he refers to 'the anachronism of my own father's writing', using terms like 'jaded' and 'faded' to describe it![2] So Ginsberg sought a different, more suitable literary father than Louis, and he found several, as we shall see.

Another early obstacle for Ginsberg was the influence of modernist writers like T.S. Eliot on his style and thinking. The modernist aesthetic dominated the first half of the twentieth century, placing a strong emphasis on difficulty,

---

[1] Bill Morgan, *I Celebrate Myself: The Somewhat Private Life of Allen Ginsberg* (London: Penguin, 2007): 62

[2] James Breslin, 'Allen Ginsberg: The Origins of "Howl" and "Kaddish"', *The Iowa Review* (1977): 82-108, 94-95

ambiguity and symbolism; its impact can been seen in the fact that a good deal of Ginsberg's juvenilia is marred by modernist inspired obscurity. T.S. Eliot was also noted for his formal expression, and this also inhibited Ginsberg, who, in the early years of his development, often affected a rather elevated tone at odds with his natural expression. The dominance of Eliot's emphasis on correct diction meant that Ginsberg 'resisted the impulse to bring [his own] poetic diction up to date'[3], and it was a while he before he found a freer poetic voice, more suited to his own informality and exuberance.

Much of Ginsberg's earliest writing eventually found its way into collections that were published after he became successful: *Empty Mirror* (1961) and *The Gates of Wrath* (1972). These two volumes include poems written between 1947 and 1952, and a number of more constructive influences on his style can be seen here. One is the American poet, William Carlos Williams (1883-1963), whom Ginsberg met in 1950. On being presented with some of Ginsberg's early poems, Williams advised him to move away from metre and rhyme towards the more natural rhythms of American speech. Ginsberg embraced this idea, together with Williams's famous dictum, 'No ideas but in things'. This is one of the key tenets of Imagism, encouraging poets to focus on concrete objects rather abstract ideas: it is based on the premise that things themselves *create* ideas. Williams's advice worked as a corrective to Ginsberg's early tendency to forgo the real world in favour of disengaged lyricism. One important poem in Ginsberg's development showing the influence of Williams, for instance, is 'The Bricklayer's Lunch Hour', included here in full:

> Two bricklayers are setting the walls
> of a cellar in a new dug out patch
> of dirt behind an old house of wood
> with brown gables grown over with ivy
> on a shady street in Denver. It is noon
> and one of them wanders off. The young
> subordinate bricklayer sits idly for
> a few minutes after eating a sandwich

---

[3] Jonah Raskin, *Allen Ginsberg's 'Howl' and The Making of the Beat Generation* (Berkeley: University of California Press, 2004): 85

and throwing away the paper bag. He
has on dungarees and is bare above
the waist; he has yellow hair and wears
a smudged but still bright red cap
on his head. He sits idly on top
of the wall on a ladder that is leaned
up between his spread thighs, his head
bent down, gazing uninterestedly at
the paper bag on the grass. He draws
his hand across his breast, and then
slowly rubs his knuckles across the
side of his chin, and rocks to and fro
on the wall. A small cat walks to him
along the top of the wall. He picks
it up, takes off his cap, and puts it
over the kitten's body for a moment.
Meanwhile it is darkening as if to rain
and the wind on top of the trees in the
street comes through almost harshly.[4]

Denver, Summer 1947
[*CP*, 12]

This began life as prose piece written in the summer of 1947, and is the literal transcription of a scene that Ginsberg witnessed gazing out of a window in Denver [Morgan, 92]. Originally he didn't think of it as poetry, but merely as a prose fragment recording a specific event. It was years later, following his meeting with Williams, that he revisited the extract and reframed it as a poem. Where Williams had initially been unimpressed by his earlier metred verse, he praised this poem highly. It is more in keeping with Williams's own observational style, and while the language couldn't be described as lyrical, the scene itself has force, particularly the image of the bricklayer putting his hat over the kitten. The rather pedestrian language used to describe the gesture is qualified by its playfulness, creating a pleasing and humorous incongruity. This is given still more force by the reference to the wind at the

---

[4]Allen Ginsberg, *Collected Poems 1947-1997* (New York: Harper Collins, 2007): 12. From here on this will be abbreviated to *CP*, and all future references will be to this edition.

end. The description of wind as 'almost harsh' seems to reflect the bricklayer's gesture, which is itself 'almost harsh' – playful, on the one hand, but an assertion of power on the other. There is a tension in the poem between playfulness and seriousness, then, and we will see this again and again in Ginsberg's work.

Another huge inspiration for Ginsberg was his great friend, Jack Kerouac (1922-1969), whose fiction draws heavily on his own life, and which mythologises personal experiences. Kerouac wrote about his friends and their lives as if they were legends, describing them with lyricism and the assumption of profundity. This encouraged Ginsberg to think in similar ways: to reflect on his own life in terms of how it might inform his art. Yet another key influence was Ginsberg's and Kerouac's mutual friend, Neal Cassady (1926-1968). Cassady was a feckless man in many ways – a petty criminal with little sense of social responsibility – but he was also a colourful character whose charisma and energy inspired both Ginsberg and Kerouac. He had a spirited and mercurial manner, reflecting an often subversive personality, shown in the way he expressed himself: in 1950 Cassady sent Kerouac a 13,000-word letter 'written in a fast paced, oral narrative style' that would influence Kerouac's own spontaneous prose style in the classic Beat novel, *On the Road*[5]. The idea of spontaneity – writing first thoughts without structure or revision – became important to Ginsberg too as it seemed to offer authenticity, immediacy and a way of capturing the instinctive mind. It is based on an assumption that reflection and editing corrupt the integrity of ideas, and that spontaneity might circumvent conventional thinking, liberating the unconscious.

Another early influence was the French writer, Jean Genet (1910-1986), whose explicit, erotic prose encouraged Ginsberg's desire to explore his own sexuality in a more forthright way: sexual candour and explicitness would become an important part of his work, and reading such writers helped him see the legitimacy and value of this. Again spontaneity becomes important here as it provides a potential way of avoiding self-censorship.

Some of these influences feature in another early poem, 'The Green

---

[5]See Steve Finbow, *Allen Ginsberg* (London: Reaktion Books, 2012): 44

Automobile', written in 1953. Ginsberg himself refers to this as a 'breakthrough poem' where, for the 'first time I let my imagination and desire dominate'[6]. In it he imagines himself and Cassady riding to Denver together:

> If I had a Green Automobile
>   I'd go find my old companion
>   in his house on the Western ocean.
>   Ha! Ha! Ha! Ha! Ha!
>
>   [*CP*, 91-95]

The laughter is indicative of the informal tone of this piece. Though it looks fairly constrained, with its use of regular four-line stanzas, it has a spontaneous feel and is much freer than his earlier metrical verse. Here we can identify the speaker as Ginsberg himself, as he fantasises about taking Cassady away from his wife and children, and the two of them embarking on a ride of the imagination. He says that, with Cassady at the wheel:

> We'd pilgrimage to the highest mount
>   of our earlier Rocky Mountain visions
>   laughing in each other's arms,
>   delight surpassing the highest Rockies

Notice the forthright way he references his relationship with another man, clearly acknowledged as sexual in the poem: 'Neal, we'll be real heroes now/ in a war between our cocks and time'. It is a breakthrough poem in terms of its emotional integrity, anticipating the candour that would become central to his aesthetic. Taking his lead from Kerouac's fictional mythologising, he sees his friend, and their relationship, in elevated terms, and this also has a spiritual dimension – 'let's be the angels of the world's desire', he says, ' ... resurrecting that lost flesh/is but a moment's work of mind'. This element of spirituality will also become a defining feature of Ginsberg's work, and it will take a number of forms throughout his career.

---

[6]Quoted in Neil Heims, *Allen Ginsberg* (Philadelphia: Chelsea House, 2005): 66

Ginsberg's Blake Vision

Some of the work collected in *Empty Mirror* and *The Gates of Wrath* addresses themes that preoccupy Allen for much of his writing life. Several poems respond to a hallucination he experienced after long periods spent reading the work of the English Romantic poet, William Blake (1757-1827), particularly poems such as, 'Ah! Sun-flower!', and 'The Sick Rose' [Morgan, 103]. He had a vivid and prolonged sense of Blake's voice speaking directly to him, later equating it to the voice of God, and assigning it deep spiritual significance. He discusses this in numerous interviews over the years, including here with Tom Clark:

> I wasn't even reading, my eye was idling over the page of The Sunflower, and it suddenly appeared – the poem I'd read a lot of times before [...] – and suddenly I realised that the poem was talking about me. 'Ah, Sun–flower! weary of time, Who countest the steps of the Sun, Seeking after that sweet golden clime. Where the traveller's journey is done'. Now, I began understanding it, the poem while looking at it, and suddenly, simultaneously with understanding it, heard a very deep earth graven voice in the room, which I immediately assumed, I didn't think twice, was Blake's voice, it wasn't any voice that I knew [...] But the peculiar quality of the voice was something unforgettable because it was like God had a human voice, with all the infinite tenderness and anciency and mortal gravity of a living Creator speaking to his son[7]

Ginsberg experienced a feeling of expanded consciousness, then, and the impression of infinite spiritual significance. This registers in early poems like, 'On Reading William Blake's "The Sick Rose"', with its references to an 'everlasting force' and 'immortality', and in a poem such as 'Vision 1948', where he addresses the 'spirit', requesting a deeper understanding of its message: 'Tell me, spirit, tell me, O what then?' While these poems lack the originality and technical skill of his later work, their sentiments are reiterated in various ways throughout much of his career, and have their origins in Ginsberg's Blake vision. He has a sense of spiritual awareness that places

---

[7]Interview with Tom Clark collected in David Carter (ed), *Allen Ginsberg: Spontaneous Mind, Selected Interviews 1958-1996* (New York: Harper Collins, 2001): 36-37

him in a Romantic tradition, and which in some ways anticipates his later interest in Buddhism. Certainly it grounds his writing in a deeply felt sense of spiritual connection, as can be seen in the piece that established Ginsberg as a poet on the global stage, 'Howl'.

The Cultural Moment of 'Howl'

In order to understand the poem that gave Ginsberg an international profile, we have to know more about its author, and the cultural context in which he worked. While Ginsberg strived to establish a poetic voice in the 40s, he also struggled with his identity and sexuality, feeling increasingly like an outsider figure in America. He had a sense of himself as a gay man, and had numerous sexual encounters with men, but just as he fought to find a suitable aesthetic, so he found it difficult to make sense of, and find appropriate ways of expressing, his sexuality. He began attending Columbia University in 1943, but his life as a student soon became turbulent, marked by periods of depression, skirmishes with the law, and a period in Greystone Park Psychiatric Hospital; indeed, it was in the latter that he encountered Carl Solomon (1928-1993), to whom the poem 'Howl' is dedicated. It was also during this period that he met many of the people who would change his intellectual and creative life. These include Kerouac and Cassady mentioned above, but also the novelist William Burroughs (1914-1997), poet Gregory Corso (1930-2001), and the street hustler and writer, Herbert Huncke (1915-1996). They are all central to what would become known as the Beat Generation; they would often feature as characters in Ginsberg's writing, taking on mythical status. Like him, these individuals were struggling to fit into American life in their own ways, and Ginsberg saw them as kindred spirits. It's their sense of estrangement, and the rejection of mainstream America, that underpins the Beat phenomenon, a movement that would have a pervasive and enduring impact on Western literature and culture.

Mid-century America was a boom period in many ways, marked by economic growth, political equilibrium, and social stability, but it was also a period associated with conformity and a conservatism that many felt was stifling and unhealthy. As Malcolm Bradbury and Howard Temperley point out, '[t]he blandness and artificial coherence of the consumer society disturbed many' in this period[8], marking dissatisfaction with the so-called American Dream, particularly among writers, intellectuals, and young people. Many have interpreted 'Howl' as an expression of that dissatisfaction, and certainly Ginsberg was aware of his status as an outsider figure during the years preceding its composition. In some ways he had been struggling against this, trying to live a 'normal' life, taking a job as a market researcher in San Francisco, for instance, and moving in with a woman, Sheila Williams Boucher. But it soon became evident that he wasn't suited to this, and he embraced a more experimental life after meeting the man who became his long-time lover, Peter Orlovsky (1933-2010). The mid 50s was a time of domestic turmoil, uncertainty, and depression for Ginsberg, created partly by his inability to find a sense of direction, or to achieve satisfaction in his love life. He referred to this period as a 'monstrous nightmare'[9], and such frustrations inevitably found their way into 'Howl', which he began writing on 25 August 1955 with the working title, 'Strophes' [Finbow, 60-61]. The early title refers to the style that Ginsberg adopted for its composition: long, prose-like lines (strophes) inspired partly by Kerouac's fiction, and partly by the letter that Kerouac had received from Neal Cassady, mentioned earlier [Morgan, 203]. Ginsberg famously performed the poem at a reading at the Six Gallery in San Francisco on 7 October 1955, to a rapturous reception. As we shall see, the poem lends itself to performance, and arguably the best way to experience it is to hear Ginsberg recite it via one of the numerous recordings in existence[10].

---

[8]Malcolm Bradbury and Howard Temperley, 'War and Cold War' in Malcolm Bradbury and Howard Temperley (ed) *Introduction to American Studies* (Harlow: Longman, 1992): 314

[9]Steve Watson, *The Birth of the Beat Generation* (New York: Pantheon Books, 1998): 179

[10]*Howl & Other Poems* (Fantasy Records, 1998) is recommended

'Howl' and Spontaneity

In interviews Ginsberg often said that he felt free to write as he liked in this poem partly because he didn't consider the possibility of it ever being published: he could be explicit, for instance, because his father would never get to read it and he wouldn't have to worry about upsetting him! This liberated him, enabling a broader palette of personal reference, obscenity, extremity, and honesty. It was a mind-set that gave free reign to the consequences of Kerouac's theory of spontaneous prose, which seeks to bypass inhibition. As an approach to writing it sanctions the uncensored voice, which is what it feels we have in 'Howl', even though the finished poem actually went through several drafts. The sense of instinctiveness and immediacy that Kerouac inspired is a vital feature of Ginsberg's aesthetic throughout his entire career – as Thomas F. Merrill says, 'Kerouac's words express the matrix of Ginsberg's abiding creative credo: 'First thought, best thought', and 'Mind is shapely, Art is shapely''[11]. As suggested earlier, according to this theory, editing and revision are damaging interventions that take poems away from the truth. As long as writing is an honest expression of the mind, then it is by its very nature art.

The impression of licence and candour in 'Howl' is compounded by the form of the poem. One of the most striking things about it, for instance, is the way it looks on the page, where Ginsberg uses long lines reminiscent of another of his literary heroes, Walt Whitman (1819-1892). Like Whitman's epic masterpiece, 'Song of Myself', Ginsberg's style is incantatory, making use of verbal parallelism: the repetition of syntactic units that build rhythm through the poem. This is one of the reasons it has so much force when it is recited: Ginsberg presents a catalogue of images and ideas that expand almost like a list, evident in the opening section with the repetition of 'who':

> I saw the best minds of my generation destroyed by madness, starving hysterical naked,
> dragging themselves through the negro streets at dawn looking for an angry fix,

---

[11] Thomas F. Merrill, *Allen Ginsberg* (Boston: Twayne, revised edition, 1988): 25

> angelheaded hipsters burning for the ancient heavenly connection to the
> starry dynamo in the machinery of night,
> who poverty and tatters and hollow-eyed and high sat up smoking in the supernatural darkness of cold-water flats floating across the tops of cities contemplating jazz,
> who bared their brains to Heaven under the El and saw Mohammedan angels staggering on tenement roofs illuminated,
> who passed through universities with radiant cool eyes hallucinating Arkansas and Blake-light tragedy among the scholars of war,
> who were expelled from the academies for crazy & publishing obscene odes on the windows of the skull,
> who cowered in unshaven rooms in underwear, burning their money in wastebaskets and listening to the Terror through the wall,
> who got busted in their pubic beards returning through Laredo with a belt of marijuana for New York,
> who ate fire in paint hotels or drank turpentine in Paradise Alley, death, or purgatoried their torsos night after night
> with dreams, with drugs, with waking nightmares, alcohol and cock and endless balls ...
>
> [CP, 134]

Also evident in this extract is how similar 'Howl' is to Whitman in terms of its use of sense units as a measure: notice how the lines often present a complete image or idea, punctuated by the repeated word 'who'. Relevant too are the principles expressed by Charles Olsen (1910-1970) in his manifesto on 'projected' verse, which proposed that 'one perception must immediately and directly lead to a further perception' [Merrill, 57]. In this way the poem is kept tight, with less possibility of the long, prose-like lines actually *becoming* prosaic. The perceptions accumulate one after another without pause or diversion. We get the impression that the poet is living it as he speaks it, rather than reflecting on the experience in tranquillity. We feel that the poet was at one with the emotion in the moment of composition, and again this is particularly noticeable in performance. The impression of immediacy is also enhanced by the fact that the lines equate more to breath-lengths than regular stresses or syllable counts. Unlike conventional, metrical verse, the line is delivered with the speaker's exhalation, measured by the duration of the breath. It's a free, natural measure, specific to the speaker and the nature of his message, rather than an inherited, prefabricated structure. This again reflects the spirit of spontaneity, drawing comparisons to bebop jazz – a form of mid twentieth-century jazz that puts strong emphasis on improvisation. Certainly the work of bebop musicians like Charlie Parker (1920-1955) and Dizzy Gillespie (1917-1993) had a strong influence on Kerouac's style, and Ginsberg's by extension. Rather than being constrained by inherited form, these musicians made music in the moment, following instinct as opposed to musical scores. Again this is in line with the idea of working free of constraint, and of writing finding its own natural shape.

'Howl' and Autobiography

I mentioned that Ginsberg exploits his own life for art, and this is another key feature of 'Howl'. The poem teems with autobiographical allusions throughout, and some knowledge of Ginsberg's life is useful to appreciate it, and indeed most of Ginsberg's writing. There are several personal references even in the short extract above, for instance, perhaps the most obvious being Ginsberg's Blake vision, referenced with the lines 'Who passed through universities with radiant cool eyes hallucinating Arkansas and Blake-light tragedy among the scholars of war'. We assume this implies that his characters share his post hallucination mind-set, and that they too are receptive to the metaphysical. Likewise, the line, 'Who were expelled from the academies for crazy & publishing obscene odes on the windows of the skull' refers to another specific incident: Ginsberg's own expulsion from Columbia University for writing 'Fuck the Jews' on the grimy window of his dormitory. So clearly he is making a personal connection here, and while 'Howl' seems hyperbolic, and often ludicrously removed from reality, it is very much grounded in the facts of Ginsberg's life. Autobiography is recast in symbolic terms and his own experience becomes emblematic of a general crisis in America. In the 'Footnote to Howl' he cites various friends and acquaintances directly by name, and he does so with reference to what he perceives is their spiritual significance: he views his friends as literally holy – 'holy Solomon holy Lucien holy Kerouac holy Huncke holy Burroughs holy Cassady'. Ginsberg and his friends (his 'generation') are presented as the angelic heroes of the poem, then, estranged victims of corrupt modern America.

'Howl' Part II: Moloch

While Part I presents examples of symbolic estrangement, Part II introduces the concept of Moloch, a biblical figure associated, among other things, with child sacrifice. As a concept in literature it features most famously in Milton's *Paradise Lost* (1667) where Moloch campaigns for total war against God, but in 'Howl' there is emphasis on Moloch as a state of mind, the cause of mental degeneration; Moloch appears to be responsible for the destruction of the 'best minds', suggesting the corrupting and debasing influence of America in mid century. Consider the following lines:

> What sphinx of cement and aluminium bashed open their skulls and ate up their brains and imagination?
> Moloch! Solitude! Filth! Ugliness! Ashcans and unobtainable dollars! Children screaming under the stairways! Boys sobbing in armies! Old men weeping in the parks!
> Moloch! Moloch! Nightmare of Moloch! Moloch the loveless! Mental Moloch! Moloch the heavy judger of men!
> Moloch the incomprehensible prison! Moloch the crossbone soulless jailhouse and Congress of sorrows! Moloch whose buildings are judgment! Moloch the vast stone of war! Moloch the stunned governments!
> Moloch whose mind is pure machinery! Moloch whose blood is running money! Moloch whose fingers are ten armies! Moloch whose breast is a cannibal dynamo! Moloch whose ear is a smoking tomb!
>
> [*CP*, 139]

Ginsberg connects the demon Moloch partly with the city and the 'cement and aluminium' of the modern, industrial world; he associates it also with the greed of capitalism and the horror of war: ('unobtainable/dollars!' and 'Boys/sobbing in armies!'). Ultimately he associates it with inhumanity and death (the 'cannibal' and the 'smoking tomb'). Moloch must be defeated if Ginsberg's angelic 'best minds' are to realise their potential. This isn't a battle that can be easily won, largely because the problem appears to exist partly within ourselves: as I suggest above, he goes on to propose that Moloch is manifest in mind – 'Moloch whose name is the Mind!' – suggesting perhaps that the demon is a feature of, or perhaps even a product of, our own thinking.

This second section is particularly confusing for readers, possibly reflecting the fact that the author wrote it under the influence of peyote, a powerful hallucinogenic drug. While the imagery is contradictory in this section, however, some critics see signs of optimism here, as Gregory Stephenson argues:

> In the pivotal section two of 'Howl', Ginsberg names Moloch as the cause of the destruction of the visionary consciousness and describes the manifestations of this antispirit, this malevolent god. Ginsberg also indicates that the Blakean 'mind forg'd manacles' of Moloch can be broken and that beatific vision can be regained[12]

It is possible to see hints at ways in which Moloch can be overcome, for example, in the final lines of the section:

> Breakthroughs! over the river! flips and crucifixions! gone down the flood! Highs! Epiphanies! Despairs! Ten years' animal screams and suicides! Minds! New loves! Mad generation! down on the rocks of Time!
> Real holy laughter in the river! They saw it all! the wild eyes! The holy yells! They bade farewell! They jumped off the roof! to solitude! waving! carrying flowers! Down to the river! into the street!
> [*CP*, 140]

As Stephenson suggests, potential 'breakthroughs' would seem to be spiritual, and associated to some extent with love and laughter. It implies, perhaps, that the way to overcome Moloch is to reject its logic via laughter, by embracing the unconventional – the behaviour of a 'mad generation' – and by privileging the spiritual over the material. Certainly any rebellion must take a spiritual form: both the 'laughter' and the 'yells' referred to here, for instance, are seen as 'holy', reinforcing the point that salvation lies in the realm of the soul. The fight will be a long haul, with victories ('breakthroughs' and 'epiphanies') punctuated by defeats, ('crucifixions' and 'despairs'), played-out as a protracted drama on 'the rocks of time'. While Stephenson presents an optimistic reading of the poem, however, some see

---

[12]Gregory Stephenson, *The Daybreak Bows: Essays on the Literature of the Beat Generation* (Southern Illinois University Press, 1990): 55

only despair in the second section. James Breslin, for instance, writes that:

> the mood here is hysterically suicidal, with anger, laughter, and helplessness combining in a giddy self-destructiveness [...] An outpouring of anger against constricting authority may be a stage in the process of self-liberation, but it is not its end; anger, perpetuating divisions, perpetuates Moloch[13]

It's true that Part II is the darkest section of the poem, and we must wait until Part III, and particularly the poem's footnote, before we can see clearer signs of what Ginsberg might be offering as an antidote to Moloch.

'Howl' Part III: Rockland

The central symbol of the rebellion, and by extension the 'self-liberation' that Breslin mentions, is Carl Solomon, the man to whom the poem is dedicated. Solomon was an American writer whom Ginsberg met in Greystone Park Psychiatric Hospital in 1949. The alternative name for Greystone is Rockland, and the refrain, 'I am with you in Rockland', pervades the final section, and has become one of the most famous lines in twentieth-century poetry:

> III
> Carl Solomon! I'm with you in Rockland
>   where you're madder than I am
> I'm with you in Rockland
>   where you must feel very strange
> I'm with you in Rockland
>   where you imitate the shade of my mother
> I'm with you in Rockland
>   where you've murdered your twelve secretaries
> I'm with you in Rockland
>   where you laugh at this invisible humor
> I'm with you in Rockland

---

[13] James Breslin, *From Modern to Contemporary: American Poetry 1945-1965* (Chicago: University of Chicago Press, 1984). Extract available here: http://www.english.illinois.edu/maps/poets/g_l/ginsberg/'Howl'.htm

> where we are great writers on the same dreadful typewriter
> I'm with you in Rockland

[*CP*, 140]

This affirms the speaker's identification with Solomon's suffering and his madness. As Ginsberg's own mother spent much of her life in psychiatric hospitals, he has an understanding of madness, and empathy for Solomon: his reference to 'the shade of my mother' is intended to make that connection. Ginsberg identifies with his psychological condition, and with his status as an outsider too: particularly, perhaps, with the idea of him as a misunderstood artist, implied by the image of the 'dreadful typewriter'. This identification hints that salvation might come via compassionate engagements with another person's suffering: those ennobling acts which humanise all parties. This notion is further suggested by Ginsberg himself in a 1989 interview with John Lofton:

> [...] the answer I was giving to the impersonality of Moloch was human sympathy. I thought that was an appropriate medicine and a positive suggestion for the culture ... It seemed to me that sympathetic attentiveness (to Carl Solomon in 'Howl') was the basic answer to the quality of dehumanisation ...
>
> [*Spontaneous Mind: Selected Interviews*, 489]

The reference to 'invisible humor' in this section is interesting too. Despite Solomon's apparent estrangement in Rockland, we get the impression that there is a degree of power in it, and that humour plays a part in an *active* rebellion against the powers-that-be. The allusion to 'invisible humor' suggests that Ginsberg's hero is laughing at the system: the line, 'where you laugh at this invisible humor', implies both an awareness of his predicament, and a capacity to mock it. He sees the humour that others cannot, perhaps, because he has insight that the majority lack. Importantly this gives him a power over his predicament, from which we might draw inspiration ourselves.

Footnote: The Spiritual 'Howl'

The footnote to 'Howl' was originally omitted from the poem on the advice of poet Kenneth Rexroth (1905-1982), but it was added later, and it acts as an effective spiritual coda to the first three sections. It can be read as an assertion of the spiritual nature of all things, a pantheistic statement reminiscent of the sentiments found in Romantic poetry, and particularly Whitman. The latter was associated with a school of thinkers called the Transcendentalists, who thought in terms of a transcendent spirit that links everything in the universe. Similar thinking can be seen in Ginsberg's footnote; notice, for instance, how it begins with fifteen repetitions of the word 'holy', developing into a list of all that is holy in the world, which includes everyone and everything:

> The world is holy! The soul is holy! The skin is holy! The nose is holy! The tongue and cock and hand and asshole holy!
> Everything is holy! everybody's holy! everywhere is holy! everyday is in eternity! Everyman's an angel!
>
> [*CP*, 142]

The implication is that spiritual interconnection might lead to our salvation – or at least to a more positive state of mind – assuming we can accept it. Ginsberg's own sense of 'oneness' began with the Blake vision mentioned earlier – it underpins the way he conceives of humanity and the universe. Once we acknowledge that everything is spiritually connected – that it's a manifestation of the divine – then we may also acknowledge our shared destiny, a shared morality, and a fundamental equality: 'Everyman', as he suggests, 'is an angel'.

This spiritual facet of 'Howl' offers an indictment of 1950s American materialism too. It was a time when the American Dream was dominated principally by ideas of economic and social advancement, and it is easy to see how 'Howl' is fundamentally at odds with such preoccupations, seeking value in the spiritual rather than the material.

'Howl', Madness, and the Id

In the broader political sense 'Howl' also subverts the kind of mid-century social conformity mentioned earlier. We can view Solomon's madness as an assertion of individualism in the face of general social compliance, a retreat from consensus reality. There is also a sense in which this subversion emphasises madness, instinctiveness, and the id, and some critics have taken issue with this, expressing a note of caution. Paul Breslin writes that:

> Ginsberg envisions a repressive social determinism so all-encompassing that the idea of individual agency is lost. The ego has been totally socialized, and only by abandonment to the involuntary impulses of the unconscious id can we act from our own motives rather than those of one-dimensional society[14].

For Breslin, the poem advocates 'abandonment' to the id, and, despite the autonomy and power this implies, there are obvious problems. For instance, Breslin goes on to criticise the social and psychological implications of such withdrawals, arguing that, once you declare a person mad, 'you deny the meaning of his resistance', and this will work to strengthen rather than undermine the status quo. This kind of criticism undermines the potential utility of Ginsberg's indictment, of course, and leaves him open to charges of toothless rebellion.

'Howl' and Humour

It could be said that 'Howl's' idealism, its apparent contradictions, its occasional obscurity, its unrelenting hyperbole, and, not least, its obscenity, demand a degree of tolerance from the reader. One way in which Ginsberg strives to win the reader over is through humour. While it deals with serious issues, it is hard to miss that many of its references and images are funny:

---

[14]Paul Breslin, *The Psycho-Political Muse: American Poetry since the 50s* (Chicago: University of Chicago Press, 1987) Quoted at http://www.english.illinois.edu/maps/poets/g_l/ginsberg/'Howl'.htm

they are often absurdly over-the-top, incongruous, or comically surreal. The critic David Perkins lists some of its comic aspects, mentioning, for instance, the comparison of 'angelheaded hipsters' to light bulbs, together with those who 'threw their watches off the roof to cast their ballot for Eternity outside of Time', and the idea of alarm clocks falling 'on their heads every day for the next decade'. These images create a patina of humour and irony in the poem, offsetting its potential high-mindedness, and outlandishness:

> Ginsberg's self-reducing humour helps to explain the remarkably good-natured acceptance bestowed on him. He is perceived more as a spiritual clown than as a threat[15]

Humour is an important part of Ginsberg's rhetoric, then, and as the poet himself said about the composition of 'Howl':

> the whole first section typed out madly in one afternoon, a tragic, custard-pie comedy of wild phrasing, meaningless images for the beauty of abstract poetry of mind running along making awkward combinations like Charlie Chaplin's walk[16]

On the occasions when 'Howl' was performed, Ginsberg often emphasised the comic elements of the poem, and audiences responded with laughter [French, 53]. In some ways, it would be hard to tolerate its ranting hyperbole for long without a degree of humour to qualify or ameliorate it – it lightens the tone of what may otherwise feel like unrelenting pontification and diatribe. But the comic elements also complement some of the poem's themes. For example, the term 'crazy' is used in the poem to refer to a state of mind – and of course mental illness is a dark subject – but the idea of cra*ziness* is very much compatible with comedy: it is in line with the comic dissent that Ginsberg seems to associate with Solomon, suggested by his laughter at 'invisible humor' mentioned above. The various humorous elements in

---

[15]David Perkins, *A History of Modern Poetry: Modernism and After* (Cambridge, MA: Harvard University Press, 1987): quoted here: http://www.english.illinois.edu/maps/poets/g_l/ginsberg/'Howl'.htm

[16]Allen Ginsberg, 'Notes Written on Finally Recording "Howl"' in Thomas Parkinson (ed) *A Casebook On the Beats* (New York: Thomas Y. Crowell, 1961): 28

'Howl' expand our sense of the comic possibilities of madness: clowns, fools, and tricksters have the potential to be both dissenting and amusing, and for all their irrationality and ludicrousness, we often associate them with wisdom. I think this is how we are meant to feel about Ginsberg's humour here. Indeed, as I suggested at the beginning of this study, we will see how Ginsberg's flair for humour remains an important facet of his aesthetic, particularly in later life as his interest in Buddhism develops.

Other Poems of the Late 1950s

Some commentators have noted that much of Ginsberg's writing strikes a very familiar tone in the late 50s, and the lesser poems appear to pale in comparison to Ginsberg's most famous piece. For some, the sheer brilliance of 'Howl' eclipses many of the poems he wrote alongside it; as Steve Finbow writes, '[t]he poetic gravity of 'Howl' pulls all in around it, sucks the life out of the lesser poems, casts them aside as sketchy husks' [76]. However, there are numerous exceptions, and many of Ginsberg's mid to late 50s poems are among his best known, and most often anthologised pieces. These include poems published with 'Howl' in his first book, *'Howl' and Other Poems* (1956), together with material included in *Reality Sandwiches: Poems 1953-1960*, published in 1963.

'A Supermarket in California'

A poem written around the time of 'Howl' is 'A Supermarket in California', a piece revealing his poetic debt to, and sense of identification with, Walt Whitman. The speaker relates a night-time visit to a supermarket where he begins thinking of Whitman and imagining the poet there with him: it makes very effective use of apostrophe, addressing Whitman as a narratee. The poem breaks into three stanzas, and in the first Ginsberg is seen walking the aisles of the supermarket 'shopping for images', which we assume means he is seeking creative inspiration. In the second he sees Whitman:

> I saw you, Walt Whitman, childless, lonely old grubber, poking among the meats in the refrigerator and eyeing the grocery boys.
> I heard you asking questions of each: Who killed the pork chops? What price bananas? Are you my Angel?
> I wandered in and out of the brilliant stacks of cans following you, and followed in my imagination by the store detective.
> We strode down the open corridors together in our solitary fancy tasting artichokes, possessing every frozen delicacy, and never passing the cashier
>
> [CP, 144]

Notice the ways in which he identifies with the long dead poet. Whitman was a gay man living in the nineteenth century, a period when such sexual preferences couldn't be openly admitted; in other words, like Ginsberg himself, he was consigned to a life as an outsider. As a gay man himself, Ginsberg is coming to realise that he'll never have the option of a conventional life. The poem implies that his affinity with Whitman puts him at odds with society, particularly via its reference to the store detective following them in his imagination. We might read the detective as symbolic of 1950s American society, with its atmosphere of oppression, suspicion and paranoia. Perhaps the detective senses their rejection of family values, and this is sufficient to cast them as potentially renegade figures? The final line of the stanza has them 'possessing' supermarket delicacies, but managing to elude the cashier, which seems like a comment on consumerism and the materialist ethos of the 50s. They are effectively stealing the food, an anti-capitalist gesture in keeping with Whitman's own anti-materialist sentiments: like Ginsberg, Whitman was of the opinion that the best things in life are free, a notion famously expressed in 'Song of Myself', with the words 'And I or you pocketless of a dime may purchase the pick of the earth'[17]. So the poem expresses affinity with Whitman's attitudes and values – they are clearly kindred spirits.

The final stanza ends on a note of uncertainty about the future, asking the question, 'Where are we going, Walt Whitman?'

---

[17] 'Song of Myself', XLVIII. The entire poem can be found online here: www.poetryfoundation.org/poems/45477/song-of-myself-1892-version

> Will we walk all night through solitary streets? The trees add shade to shade, lights out in the houses, we'll both be lonely.
>
> Will we stroll dreaming of the lost America of love past blue automobiles in driveways, home to our silent cottage?
>
> Ah, dear father, graybeard, lonely old courage-teacher, what America did you have when Charon quit poling his ferry and you got out on a smoking bank and stood watching the boat disappear on the black waters of Lethe?
>
> [*CP*, 144]

They seem consigned to a life of loneliness in a 'silent cottage', which is perhaps an inevitable consequence of their outsider status. But Ginsberg finds solace in his thoughts of Whitman, the 'old courage-teacher', who lived in an even harsher, less progressive America than the one he occupies; even with 50s conservatism and intolerance to contend with, Ginsberg has more options than Whitman would have had. Whatever future Ginsberg has, he can only suppose that Whitman had it worse: 'what America did you have', he asks, and we assume that it was one worth forgetting in the 'black waters of Lethe', the river of forgetfulness in the underworld of Greek mythology. But while the poem has a melancholic tone in parts, this is qualified once more by Ginsberg's irrepressible humour. The image of Whitman eyeing the grocery boys is funny, as is his enquiry about the murder of the pork chops; and, of course, like true trickster heroes, Ginsberg and Whitman are able to partake of life's delicacies for free, eluding the authority of mammon and the powers-that-be, represented by the cashier, and the store detective respectively[18].

'Sunflower Sutra'

One thing that demonstrates Ginsberg's maturation as a poet is his increasingly confident lineation, particularly his 'transition from the short-

---

[18]Perhaps one indication of this poem's enduring appeal is that it was used as cover art on the dust wrapper of the recent *Penguin Book of the Prose Poem*, edited by Jeremy Noel-Tod (Penguin, 2018): the cover reprints the entire poem across the back and front covers, as well as being reprinted in the anthology itself.

line form to the long, with its attendant changes in tone' [Merrill, 65]. We saw this in 'Howl', where the long line provides a fitting vehicle for the impassioned voice, with its preoccupation with madness and spiritual liberation. The poem 'Sunflower Sutra' also illustrates how effective the longer line can be in Ginsberg's hands. It describes an occasion when Ginsberg and Jack Kerouac were sitting beside a Southern Pacific locomotive, and they spot a sunflower in this landscape of industrial grime, 'surrounded by the gnarled steel roots of trees of machinery'. The incongruity is striking: on Kerouac's instruction, Ginsberg looks at the sunflower, and is captivated:

> Look at the Sunflower, he said, there was a dead gray shadow against the sky, big as a man, sitting dry on top of a pile of ancient sawdust –
> – I rushed up enchanted – it was my first sunflower, memories of Blake – my visions – Harlem
> and Hells of the Eastern rivers, bridges clanking Joes Greasy Sandwiches, dead baby carriages, black treadless tires forgotten and unretreaded, the poem of the riverbank, condoms & pots, steel knives, nothing stainless, only the dank muck and the razor-sharp artifacts passing into the past –
> and the gray Sunflower poised against the sunset, crackly bleak and dusty with the smut and smog and smoke of olden locomotives in its
> eye – [*CP*, 146]

We are immediately struck by the informality of the tone: his decision to quote Kerouac directly, for instance, suggests a readiness to dispense with the formal shaping of language one might associate with poetry. As Merrill suggests, 'Dramatic narrative enters the poem, increasing the immediacy and personal intimacy of the moment' [64]; there is no sense artifice here, and even though it's written in the past tense, we feel engaged with the event. Ginsberg describes his style in such poems in the following way:

> ellipsis in syntax – dropping of articles, connectives, sawdust of the reason – to join images as they are joined in the mind: only thus can two images connect like wires and spark ... events in time perceived, giving rise to a subjective emotion, illuminating time. A deep look ... Absolute relativity, that is, life[19]

---

[19] Allen Ginsberg, *Journals: Mid-Fifties 1954-1958*, edited by Gordon Ball (Harper Collins, 1995): 142

This technique creates a spirit of freedom in the poem: without connectives, articles and due attention to grammar, the words and phrases appear in a rush. Readers are forced to make some of the connections themselves, involving them in the process of creation, and facilitating a more personal response: what Ginsberg calls a 'subjective emotion'. Notice too how Ginsberg once more recalls his Blake vision, suggesting that the flower takes on spiritual significance for him. However, the flower exists within an industrial world that taints its natural beauty – it is 'crackly bleak and dusty with the smut and smog and smoke of olden locomotives'. No one person is solely responsible for the miserable state of the sunflower: 'The grime was no man's grime but death and human locomotives' – it has been undermined partly by the natural threat of death, and partly by the products of industry. Despite the fact that the debris of the modern world is 'entangled in [its] mummied roots', the flower still seems to retain a degree of dignity and beauty – 'there standing before me in the sunset, all your glory in your form!' Addressing the sunflower directly, he reminds it that it's not a part of the world of grime, like the locomotive, and it should be true to itself:

> You were never no locomotive, Sunflower, you were a sunflower!
> And you Locomotive, you are a locomotive, forget me not!

He goes on to make a human identification with the sunflower, then, turning it into a metaphor for all that is noble in the human condition:

> – We're not our skin of grime, we're not dread bleak dusty imageless locomotives, we're golden sunflowers inside, blessed by our own seed & hairy naked accomplishment-bodies growing into mad black formal sunflowers in the sunset, spied on by our own eyes under the shadow of the mad locomotive riverbank sunset Frisco hilly tincan evening sitdown vision
>
> [*CP*, 147]

Given the earlier reference to the Blake vision, we could assume that this identification is spiritual – a transformative 'sitdown vision' hinting at a metaphysical beauty that endures in the face of corruption. Even when that beauty appears to be tainted by the 'grime' of the modern world, it is, like humanity, 'blessed by [its] own seed'; in other words, while flesh may decay, the beauty of the transcendent spirit remains undiminished.

Again humour contributes to the informal tone. Lines such as, 'You were never no locomotive, Sunflower, you were a sunflower!' add a comic facet to the piece that is complemented by the repetition of 'locomotive', and the colloquial phrasing, 'never no'. Once more the humour offsets the potential ridiculousness and pretentiousness of the poem, but it also has another important function – humour might itself be seen as an appropriate response to the ludicrousness of the modern world. As suggested earlier, with Ginsberg there is often a sense in which humour becomes a way of reacting to life's apparent craziness, and we get that impression in 'Sunflower Sutra', created partly by the repetition of the word 'mad'. A 'mad' world demands a 'mad' response, as Warren Tallman writes:

> deepening consciousness of absurd being opens a way perception can follow and so provides Ginsberg with his best means by which to measure what he needs to know in order to be. And if you happen to be truly absurd in Madtown, what's to do, east side, west side and all around North America, but sing a mad song[20]

In other words, Ginsberg is aware of the possibilities of humour, absurdity, and the ostensibly 'mad song' as a potential life strategy: in 50s America they seem to be apposite responses to what looks like a very mad world indeed – maybe the best response to absurdity *is* absurdity itself. As we'll see often in this study, humour and craziness offer both a poetic style and a philosophical position for Ginsberg.

'America'

The idea that Ginsberg's comic absurdity is a match for America's own can be found in the poem, 'America', also published alongside 'Howl' in his first collection. Here he personifies the country, adopting his familiar strategy of addressing it directly, and listing its various shortcomings; it opens:

---

[20] Warren Tallman, 'Mad Song: Allen Ginsberg's San Francisco Poems', in Lewis Hyde (ed), *On the Poetry of Allen Ginsberg* (University of Michigan Press, 1984): 382

> America I've given you all and now I'm nothing.
> America two dollars and twentyseven cents January 17, 1956.
> I can't stand my own mind.
> America when will we end the human war?
> Go fuck yourself with your atom bomb.
> I don't feel good don't bother me.
> I won't write my poem till I'm in my right mind.
> America when will you be angelic?
> When will you take off your clothes?
>
> [CP, 154]

In some ways this reiterates the sentiments expressed in 'Howl', albeit in a less strident way. The tone is a little more measured here, but it's plainly an indictment of the country, expressing familiar themes. The speaker doesn't have a role in America, feeling like 'nothing', certainly in respect of his financial status, as the reference to 'two dollars and twentyseven cents' suggests. Again madness is an issue, with Ginsberg humorously alluding to his state of mind. America privileges the financial over the spiritual, and the speaker wonders when that might change: 'America when will you be angelic?' America is seen to lack the integrity of Ginsberg himself – while the poet became well known for stripping in public as an expression of authenticity, America is less forthcoming: 'When will you take off your clothes?' he asks it, implying that its modesty is a consequence of shame. There is a famous incident at a poetry reading when Ginsberg was heckled by a drunk, and the poet challenged him to take off his clothes. Ginsberg stripped naked, throwing his trousers at the drunk with the words, 'The poet always stands naked before the world'[21]. By implication America lacks the courage of a poet.

The informal tone of 'Sunflower Sutra' is evident again in 'America', as is the humour. The personification of America is funny in itself, with the bizarre images it creates, not least the idea of America as an entity that could actually perform a striptease! Also, the colloquial, conversational nature of the discourse is amusing: lines like 'I don't feel good don't bother me' are comically informal, creating a funny sense of a petulant speaker sulking in

---

[21]Michael Schumacher, *Dharma Lion: A Biography of Allen Ginsberg* (New York: St Martin's Press, 1992): 242

the middle of an argument. As a rhetorical strategy it is extremely effective, suggesting a non-threatening speaker who is self-deprecating and droll, rather than overtly aggressive. The humour renders the polemic more entertaining, and palatable. Later in the poem Ginsberg even offers to negotiate with his antagonist, 'There must be some other way to settle this argument', and realises that he too is a representative of America: 'It occurs to me that I am America./I am talking to myself again'. Following this acknowledgement their identities seem to merge, at least for a few lines – 'Asia is rising against me./I haven't got a chinaman's chance', and this identification with America informs the statement of personal responsibility that closes the poem, 'America I'm putting my queer shoulder to the wheel' [*CP*, 156]. This closing line implies that he recognises his responsibility as a citizen of America, but, in using the word 'queer', he makes it clear that America must acknowledge his identity as a gay man, and he will work for the country only on those terms.

While the poem is critical of America in one sense, it seems to endorse the ideal of America in another: perhaps he has in mind the ideal America enshrined in the Constitution, if not the reality of what America has become. Certainly the speaker sees America as something worth fighting for. Politically, however, Ginsberg had values not dissimilar to his mother, who was a communist: he was interested in equality and liberty, but tended to think in global rather than national terms. As Ted Morgan points out, Ginsberg as a young man believed in the possibility of progress, 'saw history as a river of development flowing steadily toward the ultimate goal of human perfection' [35], and he 'embraced the theoretical ideal of communism in his belief that democracy was only one stop in the evolution of humanity toward complete self-conscious efforts aimed at the good of all mankind' [Morgan, 35-36]. He had the view that humanity should focus its efforts on achieving utopia, then, and this broader aim is what Ginsberg might have had in mind when he committed his 'queer shoulder to the wheel'.

'Death to Van Gogh's Ear!'

Ginsberg addresses similar themes in 'Death to Van Gogh's Ear!', written in 1958, and eventually included in his third collection, *Reality Sandwiches: Poems 1953-1960* (1963). Here too there is concern for America's distorted values: what the poet sees as its materialism, hypocrisy, and spiritual sterility. The poem opens with an assertion of the transcendent significance of poetry, and a reference to the corrupted state of America: 'Poet is Priest/Money has reckoned the soul of America' [*CP*, 175]. The notion of the poet as holy is a romantic idea reminiscent again of Whitman and the philosophers who influenced him, notably Transcendentalists like Henry David Thoreau (1817-1862) and Ralph Waldo Emerson (1803-1882). In Emerson's influential essay, 'The Poet' (1844), poets are described as 'liberating gods' who can put us in touch with the eternal verities of the universe; they are seers whose penetrating vision reconnects us to the transcendent divine:

> For, as it is dislocation and detachment from the life of God, that makes things ugly, the poet, who re-attaches things to nature and the Whole[22]

Given what we already know about Ginsberg, we can see how compatible this notion is with his thinking. He too has an idea of the 'the whole', born of his Blake vision: we recall, for instance, the desire for 'oneness' evident in 'Howl', and statements like, 'Everyman's an angel!' In 'Death to Van Gogh's Ear!', the idea of the poet as priest is juxtaposed with a critique of American materialism, and the world's insensitivity to the importance of poets. He references the tragic lives of the poets Federico Garcia Lorca, Vladimir Mayakovsky, and Hart Crane, all of whom died young:

> Franco has murdered Lorca the fairy son of Whitman
> just as Mayakovsky committed suicide to avoid Russia
> Hart Crane distinguished Platonist committed suicide to cave in the wrong
>   America

Thus the poem reminds us of the poets who've suffered at the hands of

---

[22] Ralph Waldo Emerson, 'The Poet' in *Essays* (London: Ward-Lock and Co, 1911): 167-186, 174

fascism and totalitarianism: these are men of vision in Ginsberg's scheme, and, like the 'best minds' of 'Howl', they are brutalised. He goes on to criticise the writing that passes for literature in modern America, drawing a distinction between that, and what he sees as *real* poetry:

> Nobody publishes a word that is not the cowardly robot ravings of a depraved mentality
> The day of the publication of true literature of the American body will be day of Revolution
> the revolution of the sexy lamb
>
> [*CP*, 175-176]

So while literature has revolutionary potential, it has yet to find a platform. Its eventual appearance, however, will mark the day of 'revolution' for the 'sexy lamb', which may refer to those uninhibited enough to recognise and embrace the 'true literature'. Not only is the poet a priest, he is also a prophet, as suggested by the line 'I am the defense early warning radar system'. One prophesy appears to be that governments, including America's, will 'rise and fall', but that countries themselves will not. The 'good' governments don't exist yet, at least not in reality:

> But they have to begin existing they exist in my poems
> they exist in the death of the Russian and American governments
> they exist in the death of Hart Crane & Mayakovsky
> Now is the time for prophecy without death as a consequence
>
> [*CP*, 176]

Just as priests speak of paradise as attainable through the Bible and prayer, Ginsberg's poems promise salvation through poetry; they speak of our spiritual destiny. In this respect, poets such as Lorca, Mayakovsky, and Crane are martyrs to a higher truth, and Ginsberg is willing to sacrifice himself in a similar way: 'I will die only for poetry,' he tells us, 'that will save the world'. The poem concedes that, while its message is obscure at the moment, time will prove its value:

> History will make this poem prophetic and its awful silliness a hideous spiritual music
> I have the moan of doves and the feather of ecstasy

He insists that there is meaning in 'silliness', then; once more there is significance in his apparent absurdity: his comic, surreal and fantastical images and ideas. It links back to what we said above about craziness and comedy offering a strategy for Ginsberg: absurdity, or 'awful silliness', is a response to the general absurdity he discerns in modern America. Here and elsewhere he implicitly invokes the idea of the Holy Fool: the historical figure whose comedy and craziness has a religious dimension, thought to reveal a form of truth. This character type has a long tradition in Western culture as a facilitator of spiritual wisdom: for the Holy Fool comedy is a way of resisting the constraints of convention, and asserting a higher truth. As Enid Welford has written, comedy has a higher purpose in this sense:

> The theist believes in possible beatitude, because he disbelieves in the dignified isolation of humanity. To him, therefore [...] comedy is serious [...] because it is a foretaste of the truth: The Fool is wiser than the humanist, and clownage is less frivolous than the deification of humanity[23]

As someone preoccupied with the idea of spiritual connection and wholeness, Ginsberg too 'disbelieves in the dignified isolation of humanity'; rather he sees a 'foretaste of the truth' in his 'silliness' – the truth that humanity is destined to be united. When that day comes, Ginsberg's 'awful silliness' will indeed seem prophetic. In the glorious, post-revolution world, he imagines that writers and artists will occupy elevated positions:

> Vachel Lindsay Secretary of the Interior
> Poe Secretary of Imagination
> Pound Secty. Economics
> and Kra belongs to Kra, and Pukti to Pukti
> crossfertilization of Blok and Artaud
> Van Gogh's Ear on the currency

Again these incongruous job titles are comic, as is the image of Van Gogh's ear on the currency. We can see this image as a symbol of higher values, perhaps, representing the torment of the artist in a world that doesn't

---

[23]Quoted in Peter L. Berger, *Redeeming Laughter: The Comic Dimension of Human Experience* (Berlin: Walter de Gruyter & Co, 1997): 195

understand him: it becomes a romantic celebration of Van Gogh's madness, and his intense and pure artistic vision – one that transcends monetary value.

Ginsberg the Confessional Poet

Ginsberg is often described as a confessional poet. This broad term might be applied to different kinds of poetry, so it's worth saying something about how it relates to Ginsberg. It was first used in a review of *Life Studies* (1959) by Robert Lowell (1917-1977), and extended to include poets like John Berryman (1914-1972), Anne Sexton (1928-1974), and Sylvia Plath (1932-1963), together with some writers of the Beat Generation, and many others. Broadly their work was seen as different from 'the supposedly impersonal poetics of [T.S.] Eliot and [Ezra] Pound', which was more detached from lived experience, and had been the dominant aesthetic of the early twentieth century[24]. By contrast, confessional poets are generally seen as more personal, subjective, and emotionally engaged; among other things, Ginsberg shares their willingness to use the first person, and to candidly embrace personal life and feelings.

Ginsberg often claimed that honesty was fundamental to his aesthetic. In interview with the *Paris Review*, for instance, he discusses the importance of being as truthful in writing as when talking informally to friends; the poet should strive to collapse the boundaries between these forms of discourse: 'The problem is to break down that distinction: When you approach the Muse to talk as frankly as you would talk with yourself or with your friends'. According to Ginsberg, then, the writer's ambition should be 'to write, the same way that you ... are!' [Carter, *Spontaneous Mind*, 23]. Ginsberg's attitude to personal experience is rather different to that of many confessional poets, however, and this has to do with his spiritualising tendency. Matthew McNees makes this point in his study of Ginsberg's confessional sensibility, emphasising distinction between Ginsberg and poets like Lowell:

---

[24]Paul Batchelor, 'The Great Divide? Post Confessional and Language Poetry', in Eleanor Spencer (ed), *American Poetry Since 1945* (London: Palgrave Macmillan, 2017): 151-169, 151

> Instead of dwelling on personal turmoil, Ginsberg writes poems that look beyond individual problems toward a universality in the hope of gaining more freedom for more people. He attempts to transform personal issues into something spiritual so as to achieve this universality, and he locates that spirituality in the body[25]

We saw how Ginsberg might achieve such transformations from personal to spiritual in 'Howl', for instance, with its universalising tendency: the implication of his belief in spiritual interconnection is that we are all implicated in one another's suffering. And Ginsberg's life experiences are meant to be perceived symbolically: not so much illustrating a single life, as illuminating the human condition. McNees feels that this is a healthier and more useful brand of confessional writing than that produced by poets like Lowell. The fact that Ginsberg takes his life experiences beyond the self, and makes them relevant to broader humanity protects him from accusations of self-serving introspection, or poetry-as-therapy, occasionally levelled at confessional poets.

This confessional element doesn't mean that Ginsberg's work should be read as a factual account of his life, of course. We noted how Ginsberg's self-mythologising leads him to see his life in inflated, often comically exaggerated terms. Ginsberg's world is one where hustlers and criminals are considered saintly, which to some is an inversion of reality, rather than an authentic depiction[26]. Though Ginsberg's writing is founded on a belief in candour, this doesn't stop him exaggerating and idealising! His distortions constitute rhetorical hyperbole. But he, like any writer, doesn't have to tell the literal truth in order to be honest: the authenticity of the message has to do with the objective, rather than any scrupulous adherence to the details of reality. In short, while Ginsberg is often grouped with confessional poets, and almost

---

[25] Matthew McNees, *Suffering and Liberation: The Personal Poetics of Robert Lowell and Allen Ginsberg*. (Thesis directed by Drs Keith Cushman and Anthony Cuda, 2011): 83. Available online here: https://libres.uncg.edu/ir/uncg/f/McNees_uncg_0154D_10753.pdf

[26] An inappropriate tendency to romanticise down-and-outs is among the charges famously levelled at the Beats by Norman Podhoretz, a life-long critic of their writing and values. See 'The Know-nothing Bohemians' collected in *The Beats: An Anthology of Beat Writing* edited by Park Honan (London: J.M. Dents & Sons, 1987): 145-159.

all his work is to some degree related to his life, his writing is by no means always about facts, or himself in a literal sense.

'Kaddish'

Having noted the differences between Ginsberg and so-called confessional poets, we now turn to a poem where the similarities are perhaps at their strongest: his important long poem, 'Kaddish'. Ginsberg began this in the late 1950s, completing it in 1959, and finally publishing it in the collection, *Kaddish and Other Poems* in 1961. In dealing with his mother's mental illness and eventual death in an insane asylum, it explores two taboo themes common to confessional poetry; as Nicola Scholes writes:

> 'Kaddish' is typical of a 'confessional poem' in that it 'dwells on experiences generally prohibited expression by social convention: mental illness, intra-familial conflicts and resentments, childhood traumas, sexual transgressions and intimate feelings about one's body'[27]

Ginsberg saw his mother suffer from psychotic attacks from an early age, and she was institutionalised intermittently for much of her life. She was treated with shock therapy at Greystone Psychiatric Institution, and would have periods of relative calm, but home visits invariably ended with distressing breakdowns, and Ginsberg witnessed his mother in the most extreme states of trauma and despair. She was lobotomised in 1948, and Ginsberg himself gave permission for the operation to go ahead, a decision that left him guilt-ridden. Indeed some critics see elements of atonement in the poem, as well as catharsis[28]. When she finally died in 1956, Ginsberg was forced to miss the funeral, and he was upset when he learned that Kaddish had not been read at the service. Kaddish is the Jewish prayer for the dead, and the reading

---

[27] Nicola Scholes, 'The Difficulty of Reading Allen Ginsberg's "Kaddish" Suspiciously', *M/C: A Journal of Media and Culture*, 15, 1, 2012. http://journal.mediaculture.org.au/index.php/mcjournal/article/view/394

[28] See for instance Sam Clark, 'A Psychoanalytic Perspective on Allen Ginsberg's "Kaddish" (1961)'. Posted by Sam Clark on 11 August 2016 http://www.beatdom.com/psychoanalytic-perspective-allen-ginsbergs-kaddish-1961/

requires a minimum of ten men to be present, but there weren't enough. Two years later Ginsberg began the poem that would become his own personal Kaddish for his mother, and there is a sense in which he is offering the poem as an apology for missing her funeral.

'Kaddish' Part I

The poem begins with the speaker's reflections on his mother, three years after her death:

> Strange now to think of you, gone without corsets & eyes, while I walk on the sunny pavement of Greenwich Village.
> downtown Manhattan, clear winter noon, and I've been up all night, talking, talking, reading the Kaddish aloud, listening to Ray Charles blues shout blind on the phonograph
> the rhythm the rhythm – and your memory in my head three years after –
> [*CP*, 217]

It locates the reflections very specifically in time and place: New York, three years after Naomi died. He also situates it specifically in his own head – 'your memory in my head' – underscoring the subjective nature of the account, and suggesting that this poem will be as much about Ginsberg as his mother. The reference to 'corsets & eyes' creates an interesting initial image of Naomi – the drug therapy she received made her very fat, a fact referenced several times in the poem, and the mention of corsets might be an allusion to this; it may also function as a metaphor for social constraint, and the idea that in death she is finally free. In moments of madness she was also 'bulge-eyed', and references to her eyes recur later in the poem, becoming a refrain near the end. But while Naomi's eyes are gone, her memory lingers like the blues of the 'blind' Ray Charles on the phonograph.

Part I of the poem develops into a philosophical reflection on the nature of life and death, closing with the lines:

> This is the end, the redemption from Wilderness, way for the Wonderer, House sought for All, black handkerchief washed clean by weeping

– page beyond Psalm – Last change of mine and Naomi – to God's perfect Darkness – Death, stay thy phantoms!

[*CP*, 220]

Death seems almost positive here, offering redemption and the promise of comfort in the form of a home ('House sought for'). It appears to be a place where Ginsberg and Naomi might finally be together in peace – the 'Last change' for him and his mother promises the perfection of 'perfect darkness'. This is perhaps indicative of the 'destructive redemptive gestures' that James Breslin finds throughout Kaddish, and indeed in all Ginsberg's poetry. According to Breslin such gestures have their origins in a 'need to find experiences [that] shatter the boundaries of the separate self'. In this particular poem, 'Death [...] is affirmed as a release from the frustrating boundaries of the self, and as allowing a peaceful and final merge with the mother'[29]. More generally, this reflects what appears to be Ginsberg's desire for oneness and connection with all that exists beyond the self, an urge reiterated in the second part of the poem, as will be seen.

'Kaddish' Part II

Part II is the longest section, offering an account of Naomi's life and illness, and the effect it had on the family, particularly Ginsberg himself. There are several key incidents here, including one where Naomi coerced the twelve-year-old Ginsberg into helping her flee the family home, taking buses across New Jersey as she raved and hallucinated. He eventually abandoned her in a rest home, escaping back to Patterson on the night bus. 'Would she were safe in her coffin,' he says. Again this is an incident that plays on his conscience: 'I shouldn't have left her. Mad in Lakewood ... Too late' [*CP*, 222]. Another striking scene is the one where Naomi apparently flirts with her son, and Ginsberg seems to contemplate sleeping with her:

---

[29] James Breslin, 'Allen Ginsberg: The Origins of "Howl" and "Kaddish"', *The Iowa Review*, (1977): 82-107, 101-102

> One time I thought she was trying to make me come lay her – flirting to herself at sink – lay back on huge bed that filled most of the room, dress up round her hips, big slash of hair, scars of operations, pancreas, belly wounds, abortions, appendix, stitching of incisions pulling down in the fat like hideous thick zippers – ragged long lips between her legs – What, even, smell of asshole? I was cold – later revolted a little, not much – seemed perhaps a good idea to try – know the Monster of the Beginning Womb – Perhaps – that way. Would she care? She needs a lover.
>
> [CP, 227]

This graphic and disturbing scene might reinforce Ginsberg's claims to candour, of course, but some critics have seen a contradiction here – ostensibly the poet appears to be revealing intimate details about himself in the manner of an authentic confession, but the language seems chosen to deny culpability. Breslin argues that, 'the tone of the voice is noticeably more defensive than frank: he assumes an attitude of detached superiority toward the scene – idealising the act [...] performed more for his mother's emotional gratification than his. 'She needs a lover'" [99-100]. However, we could also read it as an expression of the desire for unity expressed earlier, particularly given that he follows this scene by quoting Hebrew words from the Kaddish:

> Yisborach, v'yistabach, v'yispoar, v'yisroman, v'yisnaseh, v'yishador, v'yishalleh, v'yishallol, sh'meh d'kudsho, b'rich hu.
> [which translates as 'Blessed and praised, glorified and exalted, extolled and honored, adored and lauded be the name of the Holy One, blessed be He.']
>
> [CP, 227]

The fact that Ginsberg follows the reference to incest with a quote from the prayer for the dead implies a connection between oedipal – desire and a desire for unity in death with Naomi: it's a merger that once more shatters 'the boundaries of the separate self'. An additional clue to how we might read the relationship between Ginsberg and his mother comes near the end of Part II, with the poet's allusion to a letter he received from her two days after her demise:

> Strange Prophecies anew! She wrote – 'The key is in the window, the key is in the sunlight at the window – I have the key – Get married Allen don't take drugs – the key is in the bars, in the sunlight in the window.

                              Love,
                                    your mother'
   which is Naomi –

[*CP*, 232]

Given what we know of Ginsberg, it's hard not to read the line, 'The key is in the window' as a reference to his Blake vision, with all its connotations of spiritual wholeness and merger. It hints that answers may be found in this vision, and its message of oneness with the universe, and spiritual connectedness. The poem might be seen to equate madness with a universe in which this connection goes unrecognised – the fact that we don't appreciate our oneness with all things makes us susceptible to madness.

The promise of spiritual togetherness mitigates the morbid connotations of unity in death, and the darker implications of Ginsberg's apparent obsession with this subject. The spiritual dimension of the poem is reinforced more generally in the remaining sections: between Part II and III, for instance, there is a section called Hymmnn, invoking the idea of a creator, referred to as He.

> In the world which He has created according to his will Blessed Praised Magnified Lauded Exalted the Name of the Holy One Blessed is He!
> In the house in Newark Blessed is He! In the madhouse Blessed is He! In the house of Death Blessed is He!
> Blessed be He in homosexuality! Blessed be He in Paranoia! Blessed be He in the city! Blessed be He in the Book!

[*CP*, 233]

It goes on to list the things that He has created, including homosexuality and madness, both of which are 'Blessed'. And notice how God is immanent in his creation: there is a sense in which he IS what he created, fully present in material world, in us, in the word ('the book'), and in 'Death' – it is very much a pantheistic vision, again reminiscent of Transcendentalists like Emerson and Whitman.

'Kaddish' Parts III, IV and V

Parts III and IV present more images of Naomi's madness, the latter beginning with the question, 'O mother/what have I left out/O mother/what have I forgotten'. As this section develops, Ginsberg goes on to list more details of her history and suffering, and bids farewell to them all:

> farewell
> with a long black shoe
> farewell
> with Communist Party and a broken stocking
> farewell
> with six dark hairs on the wen of your breast
> farewell
> with your old dress and a long black beard around the vagina
>
> [*CP*, 234]

The specific details are well chosen, and help reinforce our sense Naomi's history and decline in a few short lines: from her early, youthful idealism as a member of the Communist Party, to her heart-breaking abjection in later life. Thereafter the details accumulate to augment the image of his mother still further, turning eventually to the things that she has experienced, but perhaps not fully understood:

> with your eyes strapped down on the operating table
> with your eyes with the pancreas removed
> with your eyes of appendix operation
> with your eyes of abortion
> with your eyes of ovaries removed
> with your eyes of shock
> with your eyes of lobotomy
> with your eyes of divorce
> with your eyes of stroke
> with your eyes alone
> with your eyes
> with your eyes
> with your Death full of Flowers
>
> [*CP*, 235]

The mention of Naomi's eyes returns us to the image with which the poem began. Following the references to suffering and humiliation, this section closes with a positive conception of death, underscored by the flower imagery, 'Death full of Flowers'. As Merrill suggests, this can be seen as another covert reference to Ginsberg's Blake vision: 'For Ginsberg was reading Blake's "The Sick Rose" when "the voice" spoke to him' [76]. This underscores the idea of death as a release: a transition from physical torment into a blissful, spiritual union with the ubiquitous divine. The final part, V, develops the link between death and spirituality in another way:

> Lord Lord an echo in the sky the wind through ragged leaves the roar of memory
> caw caw all years my birth a dream caw caw New York the bus the broken shoe the vast highschool caw caw all Visions of the Lord
> Lord Lord Lord caw caw caw Lord Lord Lord caw caw caw Lord
>
> [CP, 235]

The final lines link references to God and a crow's caw, the latter being a sound associated with graveyards and, by extension, mortality. However, the juxtaposition implies the presence of the divine even in death: indeed, the manner of their repetition at the very end merges the two concepts. They merge phonetically, becoming a chant, and they merge in our mind, we might say, as a unification of the creator and his creation. It's a fitting close to what many consider to be among Ginsberg's greatest achievements as a poet.

Buddhism

Ginsberg travelled the world throughout the late 50s and 60s, including trips to Asia which fuelled his interest in Eastern religions. In the early 60s he gravitated increasingly toward Eastern culture, experimenting with yoga, meditation, and the teachings of Eastern faiths like Hinduism and Buddhism [Finbow, 93]. His knowledge of Buddhism in particular deepened through the 60s, and many of his poems reference Buddhist philosophy. Indeed, some critics argue that Ginsberg's post-Kaddish writing can only be fully understood with reference to Buddhism. In the early stages, Ginsberg's understanding of Buddhism seemed a little superficial and disorganised: Tony Trigilio has demonstrated how he merges Eastern religions with Western philosophy in ways that occasionally look like haphazard appropriation, ultimately arriving at a version of Buddhism that suited his spiritual needs. However, Trigilio's assessment of Ginsberg's brand of Buddhism is ultimately positive:

> Ginsberg's Buddhist poetics eludes a firm placement in one particular movement or in either conceptual pole of East or West [...] the evasions of fixed designations that mark his Buddhist poetics demonstrate the extent to which his work proceeds from the energetic confluence of body, speech, and mind emphasized in his Buddhist study and practice' – a confluence of individual self-diffusion and, paradoxically, individualism[30]

Trigilio shows how Ginsberg often struggled to reconcile, not only his ego, but his lifestyle and sexual preferences with Buddhist teachings – his status as a gay man, for instance, and his drug taking were both a source of conflict. However, he found ways of making Buddhism work for him, despite his personality and lifestyle. It has been noted, for instance, that Buddhism is compatible with homosexuality in ways that other religions are not: Trigilio makes the point that Tibetan Buddhism, of the kind Ginsberg would eventually embrace, suggests an identitylessness within which gender definitions are interchangeable, rendering the cultural conceptions of masculinity that underpin homophobia irrelevant [Trigilio, 46]. Though in the early stages Ginsberg was unfocused and uncertain in his pursuit of Buddhism, then, he matured to become a formal student, particularly under the guidance of his Tibetan Buddhist mentor, Chögyam Trungpa[31]. The main point is that Ginsberg's interest in Buddhism was much more than a Westerner's dalliance with an exotic religion: it becomes central to his life, a space where he could make sense of contradictions, both in the world and in himself, and it has a huge influence on his aesthetic and philosophy.

---

[30]Tony Trigilio, *Allen Ginsberg's Buddhist Poetics* (Carbondale: Southern Illinois University Press, 2007): 185-86

[31]For a discussion see also Marc Olmsted, 'Mind Breaths: Learning Buddhism from Allen Ginsberg', *Café Dissensus*, https://cafedissensus.com/2016/06/16/mind-breaths-learning-buddhism-from-allen-ginsberg/

'Angkor Wat' and *Planet News*

'Angkor Wat', written on a visit to Cambodia in 1963, is one of Ginsberg's most obscure poems. In an introduction to a public performance of the piece he explained its composition as 'notations taken down in the course of one night in Cambodia, in Siem Reap, which is outside of Angkor Wat'[32]. Essentially it's his response to visiting the site of the ancient Hindu temple that became Buddhist in the twelfth century. It offers a montage of images, juxtaposing descriptions of the ruins themselves with allusions to his own life, and reflections on Buddhism and other eastern religions; he also makes general observations about the country and the Far East, references to bodily decay, death, drugs, food, Hollywood, Hitler, politics, sex, and much else besides. Particularly interesting is its political dimension, and the references to the US military presence in the region:

> american husbands in sportshirts with clear,
>   bright eyes and legs spread in
>   the velocipedomotor bripping
>   on holiday from US Army Saigon
>   street hotels   I hitched
>   get polite when you'se a hiker
> 'I going to take *both* sides'

[*CP*, 317-318]

Ginsberg is ironic about being friendly with the representatives of imperialist America: he doesn't approve of the US Army's presence, but for the sake of pragmatism is 'going to take *both* sides'. Of course, as a tourist in the exotic East, his own position is ambivalent, and that ambivalence also finds expression in irony: here and elsewhere, the playful tone implies a speaker who doesn't take himself seriously. This is complemented by the fragmentary nature of the narrative, which deliberately resists coherence, hence refusing to present Angkor Wat in a reductive way: in other words, he resists what might be viewed as an imperialist interpretation of the site, or any attempt to contain, control, or, so-to-speak, conquer this spiritual place

---

[32] See Allen Ginsberg Reads at SHWU, Spoken Web. http://spokenweb.ca/sgw-poetry-readings/allen-ginsberg-at-sgwu-1969/#1

with any simple description. According to Trigilio, it represents what could be termed a surrealism of resistance: a poetics that appears to resist logic as a revolt against the discourse of reason that Ginsberg equates with conventional (and hence imperialist and capitalist) ways of communicating [Trigilio, 42].

References to an unhealthy US presence in the region parallel the references he makes to his own poor state of health: 'of stroke fear/cancer Bubonic/ heart failure/bitter stomach juices/a wart growing on my rib/Objection! This can't be/Me!' [*CP*, 314]. This implies that Ginsberg is in need of a cure, and to be returned to a purer state of health, more compatible with his ideal conception of self: the 'Me' that he presumably feels is his true self.

In amongst the often confusing montage of references and images, Ginsberg includes a 'refuge prayer'. Refuge prayers are statements expressing a Buddhist practitioner's need to move from individual practice to 'join the larger community of past, present and future Buddhists'; they represent a movement 'from self to other' expressed and enacted in language [Trigilio, 30]. Ginsberg makes an explicit reference to 'refuge' in his version of the prayer:

> ... 'I'm chasing a story'
> I'm not going to eat meat anymore
> I'm taking refuge in the Buddha Dharma Sangha
> Hare Krishna Hare Krishna
> Krishna Krishna Hare Hare
> Hare Rama Hare Rama
> Rama Rama Hare Hare
>
> [*CP*, 317]

The reference to both Buddha and Krishna conflates Buddhist and Hindu teachings, and in this sense is indicative of his rather vague understanding of Buddhism at this point in his life. However it is a significant reaching-out on Ginsberg's part to a broader spiritual community, a clear attempt to make spiritual connections beyond the self. Despite Ginsberg's superficial grasp of Buddhism, 'Angkor Wat' is an important moment in the development of the writer's Buddhist poetics: Ginsberg seems to be seeking answers to spiritual questions that have long troubled him, a need clearly articulated in the line, 'Buddha save me ... ' [*CP*, 322]. It's a strange poem, and its obscurity precludes a definitive reading, but it certainly marks an important stage in Ginsberg's spiritual striving in the early 1960s. The development of his spiritual life can be further illuminated by a discussion of another poem from this period, 'The Change: *Kyoto-Tokyo Express*', eventually included in the collection *Planet News* (1968).

The Change: *Kyoto-Tokyo Express*

Ginsberg's deepening interest in Eastern religions corresponded with his feeling that he must move on from his Blake vision, or at least from trying to recapture it. As he says in interview:

> My energies of the last ... oh, 1948 to 1963, all completely washed up. On the train in Kyoto having renounced Blake, renounced visions ... There was a cycle that began with the Blake vision which ended on the train in Kyoto when I realized that to attain the depth of consciousness that I was seeking [...] I had to cut myself off from the Blake vision and renounce it. Otherwise I'd be hung up on a memory of an experience. Which is not the actual awareness of now [Tom Clark, in *Spontaneous Mind*, 49]

The Blake vision anchored him in the past and in the abstract, at a time when he felt an increasing need to embrace the reality of the present. As we saw with 'Angkor Wat', Ginsberg also felt disengaged from the world outside his head, expressing a need to refocus on a reality beyond the self; clearly he needed to move forward both psychologically and spiritually[33].

In 'The Change' he alludes to former spiritual searches that seemed to take him away from his life, and his own physical reality. We're told, for instance, that he sought God in drugs and visions, and he speaks of 'Seeking the Great Spirit of the/Universe in the Terrible Godly/form', referencing the 'vomit & trance' of previous drug experiences. Now, however, he writes, 'Come sweetly/now back to my Self as I was – ', which suggests a different

---

[33]For more details on this see, for instance, Carl Jackson, *The Counterculture Looks East: Beat Writers and Asian Religion*, https://journals.ku.edu/amerstud/article/download/2501/2460

attitude entirely. He refocuses on the material reality of his body and his existence in the world, as suggested by the lines, 'Allen Ginsberg says this: I am/a mass of sores and worms/ & baldness & belly & smell/I am false Name ...' He posits his name, his signifier, as a fiction; rather, he locates his identity in the connection between the spiritual and the material:

> I am that I am I am the
>   man & the Adam of hair in
>   my loins This is my spirit and
>   physical shape I inhabit
>   this Universe Oh weeping
>   against what is my
>   own nature for now
>
> [*CP*, 335-336]

He follows the references to his hair and loins with a reference to the spiritual, implying that his physical shape and his spiritual shape are one and the same thing. His body, his spirit and the universe he inhabits are inextricably connected. Consider also the following stanza:

> In this dream I am the Dreamer
>   and the Dreamed   I am
>   that I am Ah but I have
>   always known

Here he collapses versions of himself in a oneness of 'Dreamer' and 'Dreamed', suggesting a self that can be 'known', but not expressed in language, a point made more directly above with the line, 'I am false Name'. The word 'Ah' is interesting too, in that it is a sound rather than a word. As Trigilio says, the use of 'Ah' here could be seen as:

> an anticipation of the important role that the *Ah* articulation, as a breath utterance, serves later in Ginsberg's career: as a mantra, *Ah* is nonsignificatory speech that performs a sacred comingling of body, speech and mind as it is spoken from the breath [81].

It is difficult to express oneself in language because language only inadequately approximates to reality, and never embodies it. There is always a disconnection between the signifier and the signified, but a mantra breaks that distinction down, merging the speaker with the utterance. 'Ah' isn't offered as a mantra in this poem, but its appearance is significant in a piece that is preoccupied with the idea of such a 'comingling' of speaker and speech; it expresses Ginsberg's desire to collapse these boundaries. Linked to this is the importance of the relationship between the breath and the line in this poem. Bill Morgan, for instance, says that:

> He followed the traditional mantric pranayamic-belly breathing cycle and hoped his readers would experience the sense of self and identity in their own bodies through breathing and cast off the metaphysical confusion of mental worlds. If read aloud, the poem was designed to cause the reader to exercise that same breathing pattern. The second section, in fact, was one big long sigh, 'OH' [376]

Here again, then, there is gesture toward 'nonsignificatory' expression as a way of 'comingling', breaking down the distinction between 'self and identity', circumventing the inevitable distortions of language. He hoped this would also extend to readers: if they were to read the poem aloud it may facilitate a connection between reader and poem, independent of language.

'Wichita Vortex Sutra'

The political concerns of 'Angkor Wat', and the interest in the inadequacies of language evident in 'The Change', combine in the superb 1966 poem, 'Wichita Vortex Sutra'. This was dictated into a tape recorder as Ginsberg travelled through Kansas in a VW bus. He composed it just as the war in Indochina was beginning to escalate: this is a war to which Ginsberg was strongly opposed, and the piece might be said to offer a poetics of resistance to the media rhetoric about the conflict. It reveals his interest in how the war was being portrayed in the media, the language it employed, and the ways in which people's opinions were being shaped. As Eliot Katz suggests, he wanted to oppose the war:

> not simply by highlighting the immorality of the war and the tragedy of massive numbers of dead persons, but also by addressing questions of

language and media in an effort to help reshape public thinking and thereby decrease public support for the war[34]

Ginsberg's recordings register a vortex of voices, with his own words competing with the language of the media, politics, telephone conversations, billboards, and so on. There is a sense in which we're offered a discourse cut off from reality, and the emphasis is on how competing voices confuse the listener, rather than effectively communicate:

> News Broadcast & old clarinets
>   Watertower dome Lighted on the flat plain
>   car radio speeding acrost railroad tracks –
>
> Kansas! Kansas! Shuddering at last!
>   PERSON appearing in Kansas!
> angry telephone calls to the University
> Police dumbfounded leaning on
>   their radiocar hoods
>   While Poets chant to Allah in the roadhouse Showboat!
> Blue eyed children dance and hold thy Hand O aged Walt
>   who came from Lawrence to Topeka to envision
>   Iron interlaced upon the city plain –
>   Telegraph wires strung from city to city O Melville!
>
> [*CP*, 402]

Notice that amid the blather of competing discourse the poets' chant is aimed at something higher ('Poets chant to Allah'); once more it is 'nonsignificatory' speech that has the potential to transport us from the confusing tangle of jabber. This hints at something that might provide hope, perhaps, an utterance offering peace amid the chaos. Ginsberg doesn't seem to trust ordinary language in this poem, feeling that effective communication resides, not in language, but in mantra. Thus he says, 'I lift my voice aloud,/ make Mantra of American language now/I here declare the end of the War!/ Ancient days' Illusion! – /and pronounce words beginning my own millennium.' [*CP*, 415]. A mantra carries more significance than mere words, rooted as it is in ancient history and wisdom. It contains elements that may

---

[34]Eliot Katz, *The Poetry and Politics of Allen Ginsberg* (Beatdom Books, 2016): 144

transcend superficial signification, and in this instance even appears to give Ginsberg the confidence to announce the end of the War! There is no indication that this might be true, or even possible, of course, and the confusing collage of discourses persists after Ginsberg's optimistic declaration. Still, the wish itself is interesting – it reminds us of the elevated conception of the bardic role expressed in 'Death to Van Gogh's Ear!', where it's assumed that the poet has insight into a higher truth. But here it is a higher truth that cannot be accessed simply via ordinary language. A refrain running through the poem is 'Language language', emphasising the ways in which language corrupts and misleads:

> Generals faces flashing on and off screen
> mouthing language
> State Secretary speaking nothing but language
> McNamara declining to speak public language
> The President talking language
> Senators reinterpreting language
>
> [*CP*, 410]

This discourse occurs in the abstract, and the voices/speakers are ignorant of the reality to which their rhetoric refers. Thus while the generals mouth language, 'Flesh soft as a Kansas girl's' is 'ripped open by metal explosion'; the hideous reality of war doesn't register in the official discourse, which is devoid of moral or emotional substance. It is mere language: 'nothing but language'.

Along with the liberating potential of chants, poetry may provide the source of another potential signifier of truth, in the form of the Chinese ideogram, as employed by poets like Ezra Pound. As Michael Davidson suggests:

> In a world so riven by undirected sound, Ginsberg yearns for a sign or an icon that participates directly in the physical character of its source. He finds it, partially, in the Chinese character for truth as defined by Ezra Pound, 'man standing by his word'.[35]

---

[35]Michael Davidson, *Ghostlier Demarcations: Modern Poetry and the Material Word* (University of California, 1997). Available at http://www.english.illinois.edu/maps/poets/g_l/ginsberg/sutra.htm

Ginsberg is drawn to the direct, unmediated nature of the Chinese character, seeing it as a more meaningful communication, at odds with political rhetoric and media distortion. This is the 'Word picture' to which Ginsberg refers here:

> Word picture: forked creature
>   Man
> standing by a box, birds flying out
>   representing mouth speech
>
> [*CP*, 408-409]

A 'Word picture' communicates with the force of unmediated truth that cannot be found in media discourse.

Another alternative mode of communication is Ginsberg's own tape recorder, which records the competing voices alongside his own, creating a heteroglossia or collage of voices. While this collage might seem fragmented and confusing, it constitutes a form of truth in its attempt to be all-embracing: it can be seen as an inclusive, egalitarian polyvocalism. As Eliot Katz rightly says:

> this technique of spontaneous recording exhibits a willingness to allow his poem to take its shape from its material, rather than to fit his observations into a predetermined formal package' [146]

Again there is an unmediated feel to this technique which enables it to evade the corrupting potential of authorial shaping.

As a whole the poem highlights and challenges the troubling deficiencies of our communication systems, which is particularly relevant to us in the twenty-first century – the era of fake news – and it feels like a very contemporary poem in this sense.

Ginsberg and L=A=N=G=U=A=G=E

The nature of American poetry began to shift in the 1960s, particularly as a response to poststructuralist/postmodernist thinking about the relationship between language and reality. Literary theory increasingly emphasised the split between the signifier and the signified, expressing views which impacted on how poets conceived of their vocation. For some it called the whole enterprise of traditional poetry into question, and occasioned a retreat into non-referential writing. Many sought an aesthetic that didn't make artificial gestures towards the real world, and began using language in ways that foregrounds its own materiality. Increasingly the emphasis was on the role of the reader in the creation of meaning, shifting the focus away from the author as creator. In the early 1970s poets associated with this kind of thinking became known as the Language Poets, taking their name from a magazine edited by Charles Bernstein (1950-) and Bruce Andrews (1948-) (L=A=N=G=U=A=G=E). Many critics feel that Ginsberg distanced himself from this movement:

> Ginsberg resisted the influence of language poetry, preferring the Beat inspired verse of Antler, Anne Waldman, Andy Clausen and David Cope [...] Ginsberg's work [...] remains the bright flare out of modernism, closer to the sincerity of the objectivist poets, the phraseology of Imagism, and the psychological honesty of confessional poets Robert Lowell, John Berryman, and Ann Sexton ...
>
> [Finbow, 96]

This is true, to a degree. Certainly Ginsberg's work invariably makes direct references to reality, particularly his own life, of course, but also to current affairs, as seen in the three poems we have just addressed. However, those poems also demonstrate Ginsberg's mistrust of language, both as a communicative medium, and as a route to spiritual fulfilment, and that mistrust suggests affinities with the Language Poets, and certainly with postmodernism, as will be seen when we address his later work.

Mantras and chanting

Despite his mistrust of language, at heart Ginsberg favoured a poetics that enabled a degree of engagement with the world, and with the self; his particular interest is in unifying reality, self, and spirit. As we saw with 'Wichita Vortex Sutra', he sees mantras and chanting as having potential in this regard. Ginsberg defined a mantra as follows:

> a short magic formula usually invoking an aspect of the Divine, usually given as a meditation exercise by guru to student, sometimes sung in community or 'kitran' – the formula is considered to be identical with the god named, and have inevitable power attached to its pronunciation. Oft used in chanting or invocation[36]

Chanting mantras became a large feature of his public performances, and he would often chant to ease tensions during heated demonstrations and moments of crisis. For Trigilio, Ginsberg's use of mantra was part of an 'effort to write a poetry of sacred experience in an emerging contemporary, postmodern landscape that increasingly distrusted linguistic referentiality' [87]. So, like Language Poets and postmodernists, Ginsberg was aware of the instability of language, and as a consequence was drawn to the mantras because they appear to offer an unshakeable link between utterance and meaning.

Ginsberg sometimes used the Buddhist mantra, *Om Mani Padme Hum*, in his writing. This is quite tricky to translate into English, and it is only possible to offer crude approximations: the sound *om* is often thought to represent the fundamental sound of all creation – the primordial sound – and chanting it can help practitioners overcome pride. *Mani* dissolves jealousy, *padme* dissolves judgemental tenancies, *hum* helps practitioners relinquish attachment to hatred. Chanting this is meant to help practitioners facilitate the development of innate wisdom, and hence enlightenment.

Ginsberg's 1971 piece, 'Hum Bom!', is a well-known example of a poem which exploits the possibilities of chanting, playing on phonetic similarities between *hum* and whom:

> Whom bomb?
> We bomb them!
> Whom bomb?
> We bomb them!

---

[36] Quoted in Paul Carroll, 'I lift my voice aloud,/Make Mantra of American language now ... /I Here Declare the End of the War!' in Lewis Hyde (ed), *On the Poetry of Allen Ginsberg* (Ann Arbor: University of Michigan Press, 1984): 292-314, 293

Whom bomb?
We bomb them!
Whom bomb?
We bomb them!

[*CP*, 576]

The 'whom' repetition provides the rhythm for the poem, and the reiterated question takes on the quality of a mantra, with the sound grounding both the poem and the speaker. The phonetic allusion to *hum* is apposite, of course, given the traditional meaning of that sound, and the idea of jettisoning hatred. The original version of the poem closes with the following stanza:

Whom bomb?
We bomb you!
Whom bomb?
We bomb you!
Whom bomb?
You bomb you!
Whom bomb?
You bomb you!

[*CP*, 576-577]

The final line underscores the self-destructive nature of hatred and aggression, in keeping with the spirit of the mantra, and the meaning of *hum*.

Chanting and Carnival: 'Thoughts Sitting Breathing'

His 1973 poem 'Thoughts Sitting Breathing' is another well-known chant piece, this time explicitly constructed around the Buddhist mantra. Each line is introduced with a syllable from the mantra. The first stanza begins 'OM – the pride of perfumed money, music food from China, a place to sit quiet', and then proceeds through the syllables of the mantra, ending:

HUM – the pigs got rocks in their head, CIA got one eye bloody mind tongue, fiends sold my phonograph TV set to the junkman, Hate that

dog shat my rug, hate Gook Heaven, hate them hippies in Hell
stinking Marijuana smog city

[*CP*, 597]

The second and third stanzas do the same, the mantra acting as a structuring device for each stanza. After alluding to numerous personal and political problems, the final stanza offers a rather scatological solution to these problems, and begins:

HUM – I shit out my hate thru my asshole, My sphincter loosens the void, all hell's legions fall thru space, the Pentagon is destroyed

This earthy image advocates letting go, as in the act of defecation. Principally the speaker strives to let go of his own hate, in keeping with the Buddhist idea of egolessness. To jettison the hate within is to liberate the self, and redeem the world – certainly a moral redemption is suggested by the line, 'the Pentagon is destroyed'. The stanza continues for several lines before closing with a celebration of 'Causeless Bliss', a phrase that is reiterated throughout the poem, suggestive of the enlightenment achievable via the kind of 'letting go' Ginsberg strives for here.

The scatological references in this poem are typical of Ginsberg's willingness to address all aspects of the self without squeamishness, embarrassment, or apology. This is often a source of humour in the poems, and could be described as carnivalesque. This term is applied to the low humour that Mikhail Bakhtin identified in the work of the French writer Rabelais (1494-1553). It is humour manifest historically in carnivals, often focusing on the body, and employing elements of obscenity, grotesquery, and extremity that would ordinarily be considered tasteless. Carnival is at odds with hierarchy, eschewing the orders of taste, beauty, politeness and decorum that civilised society demands. It has a subversive dimension, then, qualifying the authority of appropriateness, propriety and order. It's a mode of humour associated with ordinary people, as opposed to the powers that be: a folk humour that seeks to reduce all to its own level. With Ginsberg, it's often posited as a corrective to his own sense of status – a self-deflating humour that might usurp the authority of his own ego. In this poem, the uninhibited references to the body complement the mantra and its ability to focus the individual *on* the body, breaking down the distinction between the fictional ego and the material self in all its corporeality.

Ginsberg's references to sex also often have a carnivalesque feel. In this poem he mentions his 'Lust in heart for the pink tender prick'd school-boy upstairs bedroom/naked with his books', where Ginsberg effectively admits his taboo desire for underage boys. And he mentions too the fact that 'Everyone I fucked/is dead and gone – everyone I'm gonna fuck is turning to a ghost' [*CP*, 597-599], linking two taboos, sex and death, together in a union that suggests the transient nature of both desire and flesh. Carnival – with its emphasis on the uninhibited bodily connection – links the individual with the masses at a corporeal level, asserting one's status as part of a larger whole. In other words, it's another expression of connection with the world beyond himself. As Peter Jones writes, the carnival attitude facilitates 'loss of self in an experience of communion, as opposed to a Kantian-bourgeois aesthetic of individualistic and reasoned pleasure'[37]. In other words, Ginsberg's carnival humour, both in its scatological and sexual nature, can be seen to complement his need to relinquish his identity in keeping with his developing Buddhist inclinations. We might also view it as evidence of the utopian desire for connection seen elsewhere in his work. The implication is that individuals, society, and the Pentagon would do better to acknowledge their human connection, and a good place to start is by admitting to the existence of their own shit, letting it 'fall thru space' with their hate!

'Mugging'

One of Ginsberg's best-known poems to reference chanting is the 1974 piece, 'Mugging', where he describes being mugged near his apartment in Manhattan. It's a wonderfully detailed poem that creates a strong sense of place, describing Ginsberg walking out on a late autumn evening, and encountering a gang of youths on a street corner. One puts an arm around him, while another trips him, and he is dragged into a derelict shop. His

---

[37]Peter Jones, 'Anarchy in the UK: '70s British Punk as Bakhtinian Carnival', http://pcasacas.org/SiPC/24.3/Jones.htm

response is to begin chanting:

> as I went down shouting Om Ah Hum to gangs of lovers on the stoop watching
> slowly appreciating, why this is a raid, these strangers mean strange business with what – my pockets, bald head, broken-healed-bone leg, my softshoes, my heart –
> Have they knives? Om Ah Hum – Have they sharp metal wood to shove in eye ear ass? Om Ah Hum
>
> [*CP*, 633]

Here the chant is less a part of the structure of the poem, and more a subject of the poem. In a sense it explores whether Ginsberg's chanting method can survive an encounter with harsh reality, and it doesn't. Certainly the youths aren't calmed by it, rather they threaten to kill him if he doesn't stop chanting, which adds a delightful comic dimension to the piece, despite the seriousness of the subject. 'Shut up or we'll murder you' – 'Om Ah Hum, take it easy' [*CP*, 634]. Part I of the poem ends with the assailants leaving, and a reference to the inadequacy of his chant:

> as I rose from the cardboard mattress thinking Om Ah Hum didn't stop em enough,
> the tone of voice too loud – my shoulder bag with 10,000 dollars full of poetry left on the broken floor –
>
> [*CP*, 634]

Part II describes him going back to the scene with a policeman, and then being joined by the 'Neighbourhood street crowd' who claim not to have seen anything. It ends with a reference to the neighbourhood's decay, and the residents' poverty and suspicion of the police. There is no sense of community in the neighbourhood, and Ginsberg's chant looks comically futile in this scene of urban decay and social disintegration. Ginsberg measures his idealistic philosophy against reality, then, and finds humour as its shortcomings are exposed. But the final irony is that the muggers overlook the items of true value – the 'shoulder bag with 10,000 dollars full of poetry' – and this allows Ginsberg the last and longest laugh.

Cosmopolitan Comedy: Zen and Humour

We have seen how Ginsberg frequently uses humour in his work: it is a key feature of his writing throughout his career, but it takes on a deeper significance as his interest in Buddhism increases. Humour has a special place in Buddhism, particularly in Zen Buddhism, and while Ginsberg didn't practise Zen as such, several commentators have noted the spirit of Zen in his work, and Ginsberg himself had an understanding of Zen, and an interest in it.[38] There is very often a Zen feel to Ginsberg's humour, particularly notable in one of his late poetry collections, *Cosmopolitan Greetings* (1994). This was published at a time when the aging poet's ideas about Buddhism were well formed, and the year in which he wrote a foreword to a collection of Zen poems by Ko Un: *What? 108 Zen Poems*. In this foreword he makes the point that, while he hasn't experienced Zen Practice himself, he, like 'everyone eastern-literate knows the taste of koan & haiku, & gatha and doha nonconceptual riddles – or conceptions that annul conceptual speculation'[39]. As we shall see, Ginsberg's poems often betray a 'taste of koan' – those humorous Zen riddles that expose the limitations of logic – giving full reign to his trickster persona.

According to Conrad Hyers, humour has numerous important roles in Zen Buddhist philosophy and method, working to expose the folly of 'the ego and its desires and attachments'[40]. Humour can be used 'as a technique for reversing and collapsing categories', 'as a technique for embracing opposites', and, 'as an expression of enlightenment, liberation, and inner harmony'.[41] To illustrate this, Hyers relates a Zen anecdote in which a dying

---

[38] Tony Trigilio sees the spirit of Zen in 'the relationship between Eastern thought and the European Surrealist/Dadaist avant garde that Ginsberg established in 'Angkor Wat' [Tony Trigilio, *Allen Ginsberg's Buddhist Poetics* (Southern Illinois University Press, 2007): 43]. This poem certainly suggests a penchant for the absurd compatible with Zen thinking. It is compatible too with Chögyam Trungpa's notion of Crazy Wisdom, which has affinities with Zen (see note 47).

[39] Allen Ginsberg, Foreword to Ko Un: *What? 108 Zen Poems* (Berkeley: Parallax Press, 1997): 10

[40] Conrad Hyers, *The Laughing Buddha: Zen and the Comic Spirit* (Wolfeboro, NH: Longwood Academic Press, 1989): 55

[41] Conrad Hyers, 'Humour in Zen: Comic Midwifery', *Philosophy East and West*, Volume 39, no. 3, July 1989: 267-277, 270

master offers words of wisdom to his monks. After telling them that 'Truth is like a river', the puzzled monks ask him, 'Master, what do you mean, "Truth is like a river"?' Wearily the master opens his eyes and in a weak voice whispers, 'OK, Truth is not like a river' ['Comic Midwifery', 271]. Hyers sees this as a Zen

> attempt to demonstrate the equivalence of alternative philosophical positions and countering each by the other, to reduce alternative philosophical positions to an absurdity. The intent is [...] to point up the absurdity in trying to grasp after and cling to reality by means of this or that philosophical position
>
> ['Comic Midwifery', 271]

Such efforts to collapse categories and embrace opposites appear throughout *Cosmopolitan Greetings*. In 'Hard Labor', for instance, Ginsberg juxtaposes opposing alternatives in a very obvious way:

> After midnite, Second Avenue horseradish Beef
>   at Kiev's wood tables –
> The Kasha Mushrooms tastes good
>   as Byelorussia usta when my momma
>   ran away from Cossacks 1905
> Did the 5 year plan work? How bad Stalin?
> Am I a Stalinist? A Capitalist? A
>   Bourgeois Stinker? A rotten Red?
> No I'm a fairy with purple wings and white halo
>   translucent as an onion ring in
> the transsexual fluorescent light of Kiev
>   Restaurant after a hard day's work
>   *February 17, 1986, 12:35 a.m.*
>   [*CP*, 948]

Here the political narratives of capitalism and communism are juxtaposed, implicitly offsetting one another in their extremity. The speaker is neither 'Bourgeois Stinker [nor] rotten Red', but an apolitical angelic 'fairy'! Ginsberg renders extreme political ideologies absurd, in a sense, and at the same time he renders *himself* absurd, as a 'fairy with purple wings and white halo'. The spiritual imagery elevates him above the concerns of corrupt political systems, and indicts them, but the deliberately ridiculous aspects of the angelic image qualify any sense of his own superiority. The repetition of the prefix 'trans', meanwhile, reinforces the poem's challenge to polarizing categories and reductive definitions. In the 'transsexual fluorescent light' which frames Ginsberg's self-definitions, then, either/or categories are not applicable, regardless of whether they relate to political philosophies, or Ginsberg's own sexuality. The poem perfectly illustrates the philosophical 'equivalence' that Hyers mentions.

According to Hyers, a key hierarchy that Zen humour attacks is the one between the sacred and the secular: 'anything, however holy, is potentially an idol', and Zen humour acts as a corrective to that, ensuring that no 'aspect of one's existence is to be elevated beyond the requirements of humour' [*The Laughing Buddha*, 55]. Ginsberg demonstrates his capacity for this kind of comic profanation in the poem 'Everyday', cited here in full:

> The Lama sat
>   in bed
> with bamboo
> backscratcher
> his false teeth
> in a big
> glass of water
> on the sunny
> windowsill.
>
> [*CP*, 1042]

Here Ginsberg asserts the everydayness of the Lama, undermining any sense of his elevated status with the very human image of his false teeth in a glass of water. The fact that it's a 'big' glass of water augments the incongruity of the image, and the comedy, as does the phonetic linking of 'big' with 'bed/ ... bamboo/backscratcher'. The humour demonstrates a Zen-like contention that 'the master is not sacrosanct' [Hyers, *Laughing Buddha*, 64], and develops out of a perspective that transcends the perceived distinction between the sacred and the secular. It is a kind of democratisation, completely at odds with hierarchy.

In his discussion of Zen humour, the philosopher John Morreall says that:

the experience of enlightenment, with its sudden realisation of the illusory nature of the self, can itself be a profound kind of amusement. The biggest joke I shall ever experience is me. And once I am liberated from attachment to my ego and see myself with humour, the humour in all experience comes easily[42]

Likewise, Hyers argues that Zen life and teaching often focuses on 'comic reversals' where 'all categories are turned upside down, and thus relativized and finally collapsed [...] challenging the whole valuational structure of the discriminating mind' ['Comic Midwifery', 272]. Again such reversals can be seen often in *Cosmopolitan Greetings*; consider, for instance, the short poem, 'Proclamation', dedicated to Carlos Edmondo de Ory, included below in full:

I am the King of the Universe
I am the Messiah with a new dispensation
Excuse me I stepped on a nail.
A mistake
Perhaps I am not the Capitalist of Heaven.
Perhaps I'm a gate keeper snoring
    beside the Pearl Columns –
No this isn't true, I really am God himself.
Not at all human. Don't associate me
    w/that Crowd.
In any case you can believe every word
    I say

October 31, 1987
Gas Station, NY
[*CP*, 971]

Here the speaker asserts that he is God, an idea comically undermined when he steps on a nail, and further qualified as he begins to question his own status. When he reasserts it ('No ... I really am God'), his claim, together with his request not to be associated 'w/that Crowd', is rendered absurd, and potentially comic. The mortal and the divine are relativized, then, and the final statement, 'you can believe every word/I say', becomes ironic. In

---

[42]John Morreall, *Comic Relief: A Comprehensive Philosophy of Humor* (Chichester: Wiley-Blackwell, 2009): 137

this poem, Ginsberg creates a 'God' that can only be known through the word, and at the same time reminds us of the inevitably ambiguous nature of words: we cannot, of course, believe *anything* he says.[43] Thus there are two inversions going on here: God potentially becomes man, collapsing those categories of mortal and divine, and the truth potentially becomes a lie, collapsing those categories also. Things have the capacity to become their opposite, and hence one can't have faith in anything the speaker, or anyone else says. It's this indeterminacy that lies at the heart of Ginsberg's humour, and which, to use Hyer's terms, relativizes and collapses categories.

Ginsberg the Zen Trickster

There is indeterminacy too in his poem 'Salutations to Fernando Pessoa' where he presents a mock attack on the famous Portuguese poet, denigrating his achievement in relation to his own:

> Every time I read Pessoa I think
> I'm better than he is I do the same thing
> more extravagantly – he's only from Portugal,
> I'm American greatest Country in the world
> ....
> What way'm I better than Pessoa?
> Known on 4 Continents I have 25 English books he only 3
> ....
> As a Buddhist not proud my superiority to Pessoa
> I'm humble Pessoa was nuts big difference
> ....
> I'm speaking seriously about me & Pessoa.
> Anyway he never influenced me, never read Pessoa
> before I wrote my celebrated *Howl* already translated into 24 languages ...
> ....
> diarrhea mouth some people say – Pessoa Schmessoa
>
> [*CP*, 976-977]

---

[43] He hints perhaps at the Zen notion of the 'wordless dharma'; the idea that, in Hyers' words, 'The final word is silence, pregnant with meaning.' (*Laughing Buddha*, 141).

The speaker's self-praise and the criticisms of Pessoa are absurd and hyperbolic enough to signify ironically, but elsewhere in the poem, to underscore the point, he claims that one of the reasons he is better than Pessoa is because his rival was shorter than he is! He ends by calling him 'diarrhea mouth', and exclaiming 'Pessoa Schmessoa'. Ginsberg presents a list of his own 'better' achievements as a poet, but these apparently boastful assertions arguably deconstruct themselves in a manner that might negate rather than boost the ego. Even if they *are* the product of genuine feelings of superiority, putting his conceit on show reveals his human fallibility in a way that arguably qualifies the boast. So is he being boastful or modest? Ultimately it's impossible to know for sure how the assertions relate to Ginsberg the man: in a sense it is neither self-praise nor self-criticism, but both, once more denying the possibility of an either/or reading. Again, in the spirit of Zen, things have the capacity to become their opposite.

Such uncertainty is frequently complemented by a playful, humorous tone in his writing, but there is often a degree of uncertainty about the existence of humour itself. While humour is undoubtedly present in parts, it is by no means easy to determine how it signifies, or even if we should find his lines funny at all. Ginsberg's poetry teems with incongruities, but while all humour contains incongruity, not all incongruities are humorous: according to most theories of humour, there needs to be an element of resolution to the incongruity for it to signify humorously. Søren Kierkegaard, for instance, deemed comedy the 'painless contradiction' precisely because it is born of *resolvable* contradictions: 'the comic apprehension evokes the contradiction or makes it manifest by having in mind the way out'[44]. The 'way out' of the contradiction is provided by the humour itself, which offers a justification or reason for it: in other words, we allow and feel comfortable with contradictions *when they are funny*. However, importantly, contradictions and incongruities that *aren't* funny merely make us uncomfortable. This is crucial because we can't always tell if Ginsberg is trying to be funny or not: in other words, his work tends not to supply this 'way out' in any obvious

---

[44]Søren Kierkegaard, 'Concluding Unscientific Postscript', in John Morreall (ed), *The Philosophy of Laughter and Humor* (New York: State University of New York Press, 1987): 83-4

sense, and often resides in the realm between humour and seriousness. Ginsberg has been compared to the Trickster Hero, a comparison he makes himself in interview where he identifies with the mythical figure who operates 'twixt earnest and joke'.[45] This is exactly the tone of much of his poetry here; it's a trickiness that parallels his willingness to embrace contradiction.[46] It finds explicit expression in the poem which prefaces *Cosmopolitan Greetings*, 'Improvisation in Beijing'. Here he reinforces his readiness to embrace opposites with reference to Walt Whitman's famous statement about contradiction: 'I write poetry because Walt Whitman said, "Do I contradict myself?/Very well then I contradict myself (I am large, I contain multi-/tudes.)"'. In the penultimate line of the poem he challenges the logic that might impede the poet's inclination to flout reason in this way: 'I write poetry because no reason no because' [*CP*, 939]. Here reason's demand for a logical ending to this sentence is ignored, creating the potential for humour ('because no reason no because'); however, it doesn't necessarily signify as humorous: unlike in a conventional joke, there is no context to signal humour (no verbal cues designed to invite us to receive that statement in a humorous way); indeed as an implicit challenge to structures of reason, it is potentially unsettling rather than humorous.[47] Unresolved incongruities are associated with cognitive dissonance, and as such are perceived as threatening and unwelcome rather than funny. This makes for an ambiguity in Ginsberg's writing that is sometimes humorous, and sometimes unsettling, creating

---

[45] See for instance his 1994 interview with Jeremey Isaacs, where he answers Bob Dylan's apparent contention that he is a 'con-man extraordinaire', and claims this is a 'trickster hero' reference. It's worth noting that this interview took place as Ginsberg was promoting *Cosmopolitan Greetings*. http://ginsbergblog.blogspot.co.uk/2011/11/bbc-face-to-face-interview-1994-asv21.html

[46] For a discussion see 'The Puritan and The Profligate', John Lofton: An Interview with Allen Ginsberg, *Harper's Magazine*, January 1990. http://jig.joelpomerantz.com/otherwriters/ginsberg.html

[47] We have seen how the spirit of Zen humour resists hierarchy, and the possibility of reductive solutions. In this respect it has affinities with Chögyam Trungpa's notion of Crazy Wisdom, associated with the absence of answers: 'the point where there is no answer we tend to give up hope of an answer [...] This hopelessness is the essence of crazy wisdom', Chögyam Trungpa, *Crazy Wisdom*, Judith L. Lief, Sherab Chödzin (eds), Boston: Shambhala Publications, 2001): 10

uncomfortable challenges to logic that can sometimes deny us the compensation of humour. As in Zen humour, the onus is heavily on the reader/listener to decode it: perhaps we might even go as far as to say, it constructs a *potential* humour freed of the need to be funny; again, exactly like Zen humour as Hyers sees it, 'free of desire and attachment, or of meaning and meaninglessness' [*The Laughing Buddha*, 168].

In his discussion of humour as a technique for embracing opposites, Hyers notes how Zen often yokes together seemingly incompatible identities: 'as in the case of the Chinese monk who wore a Buddhist robe, a Confucian hat, and Taoist sandals as a way of breaking out of religious stereotypes and labels, confusing and confounding fixed identities [...] Reality, Truth, Wisdom – these cannot be imprisoned in the pigeonholes of ordinary consciousness' ['Comic Midwifery', 273]. Perhaps the clearest expression of this in *Cosmopolitan Greetings* is the poem 'Yiddishe Kopf', where Ginsberg offers a series of reasons why he is Jewish:

> Jewish because Buddhist, my anger's transparent hot air, I shrug my
>   shoulders.
> Jewish because monotheist Jews Catholics Moslems're intolerable
>   intolerant –
>
> [*CP*, 1013]

There is a collapsing of Jewish/Buddhist/Muslim/Catholic identities here that sees Ginsberg 'confusing and confounding fixed identities' in the Zen tradition. The notion of his Jewishness being dependent on his Buddhism (suggested by the word 'because') creates another unresolved incongruity, once more flouting logic in a way that is both potentially humorous, and simultaneously confusing. Though it has humorous potential, the fact that the grounds for linking Jewishness and Buddhism are unexplained and apparently irrational, complicates the tone, 'frustrating and confounding ... the intellect' [Hyers, *The Laughing Buddha*, 151]. Not only does he confuse fixed identities, then, confusion is part of his aesthetic, once more creating a space where reason is suspended, and irrationality isn't necessarily made safe by humour. But it is the reader rather than the speaker who is potentially 'frustrated and confounded' here: the speaker's decision to 'shrug [his] shoulders', while suggesting confusion, also suggests a willing acceptance of that confusion.[48]

Carnival Again: 'Sphincter'

This notion of acceptance brings us to Hyers' third category of Zen humour, 'as an expression of enlightenment, liberation, and inner harmony', which, according to Hyers, is the 'higher, nonfunctional level of humour where humour exists for itself and not just in the service of some other end'. Where humour is usually 'an expression of tension ... created by dualities, discriminations, and oppositions of various sorts [...] humour at its highest and fullest [...] arises, not out of inner tension, but inner harmony' ['Comic Midwifery', 274]. We occasionally find hints of such harmony in the various trickster-like evasions of hierarchy and definition seen above, but it can also be seen clearly in a poem like 'Sphincter', where Ginsberg collapses another opposition, this time between interior and exterior. The poem is included here in its entirety:

> I hope my good old asshole holds out
> 60 years it's been mostly OK
> Tho in Bolivia a fissure operation
>   survived the *altiplano* hospital –
> a little blood, no polyps, occasionally
>   a small hemorrhoid
> active, eager, receptive to phallus
>   coke bottle, candle, carrot
>   banana & fingers –

---

[48] It's worth mentioning that years earlier, in a first version of a poem called, 'Kral Majales' (King of May), Ginsberg presented a similar collapsing of apparently distinct identities, claiming that he is the 'King of May', because 'I am of Slavic parentage and a Buddhist Jew' [Ginsberg, *Collected Poems: 1947-1980* (New York: Harper & Row, 1984): 354]. In 'Return of Kral Majales' written in 1990, he develops this still further, both inverting and embracing opposites in a manner exactly like that which Myers identifies, 'confounding fixed identities': He is the King of May, he tells us, with a 'paper/crown' and 'high blood pressure, diabetes, gout, Bell's palsy, kidneystones, & calm eyeglasses'(*CP*, 984): in other words, both a king, and the inversion of a king.

>   Now AIDS makes it shy, but still
> 	 eager to serve –
>   out with the dumps, in with the condom'd
> 	 orgasmic friend –
>   still rubbery muscular,
> 	 unashamed wide open for joy
>   But another 20 years who knows,
> 	 old folks got troubles everywhere –
>   necks, prostates, stomachs, joints –
> 	 Hope the old hole stays young
>   till death, relax
>
> [CP, 950]

Here we again see Ginsberg's fondness for carnival humour. He employs what Bakhtin would call a 'carnival semiotics' – a disruption of conventional signification – that breaks down the distinction between inside and outside the body. To quote Bakhtin:

> The main principle of the official semiotics of the body is the concealedness of the body's insides. By contrast, carnival semiotics allows the inner realm to enter eccentrically into the outside world and vice versa: it stages the penetration of the outside into the bodily insides as a spectacle. The boundary marking the division between the body's insides and outside is suspended through the two movements of protruding and penetrating[49]

This is precisely what happens in Ginsberg's poem: 'carnival semiotics' undermines the official semiotics of inside/outside; in other words, 'the official semiotics' of the body's 'concealedness' is undermined as we see his blood, shit and haemorrhoids; things that are conventionally kept apart are embraced on equal terms, 'unashamed' and 'wide open'. Whilst on the one hand he presents himself as amenable to desire, the references to age and decay create a self-mocking contrast, implying the persona of one who has, to quote Hyers, 'learned to laugh at the folly of the desiring self' [*The Laughing Buddha*, 117]. There is a sense in which, whilst acknowledging desire, Ginsberg's refusal to take desire seriously maintains a 'Zen emphasis upon

---

[49]Mikhail Bakhtin, *Rabelais and his World*, translated Helene Iswolsky (Bloomington: Indiana UP, 1984): 150-51

non-attachment' [118]. It achieves balance rather than tension, expressing an inner harmony and a spirit of contentment underscored by the final word: 'relax'. Like most of the poems in *Cosmopolitan Greetings*, its theme is informed by a potential humour that is contradictory and, for that reason, evasive: yoking together desire and death, sex and excrement, joy and aids, orgasm and pain, old and young, creates a shifting tone and focus that resists resolution, and cannot be comfortably categorised *as* humour. It is also ambiguous as a statement of desire: rather than embracing or denying desire, the emotion itself is rendered ludicrous, and we have the impression that Ginsberg is neither attached to desire, or the desire to relinquish desire; in other words, an 'inner harmony' prevails!

Ginsberg's perception of himself as occupying the realm 'twixt earnest and joke' is crucial, then, and particularly interesting with regard to how Ginsberg's humour might relate to his ego. Indeterminacy prevails in *Cosmopolitan Greetings*, as do the instabilities and uncertainties that joking generates. In his writing, Ginsberg is neither Buddhist nor Jew, Capitalist nor Red, rational nor irrational, outside nor inside! While humour is certainly present in his work, it resists stability and the illusory image of a coherent self; rather, in the tradition of Zen, it emphasises 'non-attachment'; he does not grasp after the reassuring, identity-confirming closure of the traditional joke, but gestures beyond what Hyers terms, 'The abstract world of the desiring self' [*The Laughing Buddha*, 163]. In no sense can this be seen as a humour of power and superiority; rather it is more like the kind of humour that Ted Cohen identifies as born of 'a mood of acceptance, of willing acknowledgement of those aspects of life that can be neither subdued nor fully comprehended';[50] in Hyers' words, it might be considered 'a humour of acceptance of the thusness and suchness of the world, transcending the anxiety over possessing and not possessing, existing and not-existing, success and failure' [163]. Ginsberg himself might summarise his position more succinctly: 'I write poetry because no reason because'.

---

[50]Quoted in Adrian Bardon's 'The Philosophy of Humor', in *Comedy: A Geographic and Historical Guide*, (ed) Maurice Charney (Connecticut: Greenwood Press, 2005): 18, http://faculty.swosu.edu/frederic.murray/philosophy%20of%20humor_1.pdf

Dissenting Voices: Ginsberg's Detractors

Ginsberg will best be remembered for 'Howl' and 'Kaddish', and some argue that he wrote little in later life to match the scope and force of these great early poems. Indeed several critics perceive a huge decline in the quality of Ginsberg's work, not least the man responsible for publishing 'Howl', Lawrence Ferlinghetti, who described it as 'a shocking deterioration'[51]. Ginsberg's Buddhism is sometimes said to have marred his writing too. We have seen how his religion underpins his inclinations as a poet, and is a useful lens through which some of it can be read, but commentators such as Jonah Raskin argue that Buddhism 'may have given him too easy an access to readymade mythologies, beliefs and phrases' [Raskin, 228], and some of these may seem a little too convenient at times. Other critics argue that Ginsberg's writing is too facile and easily understood: Mark Ford makes this point in a 1987 review of *White Shroud*, arguing that 'His poems divulge their secrets automatically, without asking'; he claims that Ginsberg writes with a 'kind of upfrontness [that] is in complete opposition to the deep "quarrel with ourselves" which activates so much of the great poetry written since the Romantics'. So there is a superficiality about Ginsberg's poems, and 'probing beneath their surfaces reveals nothing'[52]. While Ford dismisses most of Ginsberg's oeuvre in this way, it's mainly the later poems that attract such criticism.

As we have seen with *Cosmopolitan Greetings*, however, what often redeems the late poetry is Ginsberg's ability to bring humour to bear on his subjects, and this should not be dismissed lightly. Indeed this humour is born out of exactly the kind of deep 'quarrel with ourselves' that Ford identifies in great poetry. Ginsberg's flair for humour often adds layers of complexity to ostensibly superficial poems, and 'probing beneath their surfaces' can actually prove immensely profitable. Sometimes this humour takes the form of overt political satire, as in poems like 'C'mon Pigs of Western

---

[51] Jonah Raskin, *Allen Ginsberg's 'Howl' and The Making of the Beat Generation* (Berkeley: University of California Press, 2004): 226

[52] Mark Ford, 'I am Prince Mishkin', *London Review of Books*, 23 April 1987, https://www.lrb.co.uk/v09/n08/mark-ford/i-am-prince-mishkin

Civilization Eat More Grease', included in the posthumous collection, *Death and Fame: Poems 1993-1997*. It opens with the lines:

> Eat Eat more marbled Sirloin more Pork 'n
>   gravy!
> Lard up the dressing, fry chicken in
>   boiling oil
> Carry it dribbling to gray climes, snowed with
>   salt,
> Little lambs covered with mint roast in racks
>   surrounded by roast potatoes wet with
>   buttersauce,
> Buttered veal medallions in creamy saliva,
>   buttered beef, by glistening mountains
>   of french fries

This apparent celebration of Western cuisine continues, accumulating images in the form of a list. Notice the skilful way Ginsberg undermines the appeal of such fayre, with his emphasis on excess, and references to dribbling and saliva. We are queasy before we even reach the explicitly stated consequences of unchecked indulgence:

> Diabetes & stroke – monuments to carnivorous
>   civilizations
> presently murdering Belfast
>   Bosnia Cypress Ngorno Karabach Georgia
> mailing love letter bombs in
>   Vienna or setting houses afire
>   in East Germany – have another coffee,
>   here's a cigar.
> And this is a plate of black forest chocolate cake,
>   you deserve it

[*CP*, 1071-1072]

This is a poem about the appetites and values that the West exports around the world, linked in the final lines to incidents of brutality in 'carnivorous/ civilisations'. Ginsberg's humour has most force in the closing image of the 'black forest chocolate cake' and the line, 'you deserve it'. The line is ironic, but like all irony it is slippery. While we can clearly see this as an indictment of the West (which presumably deserves its excess-related diseases), there is a degree to which Ginsberg is implicated in this narrative of overindulgence: after all, the poet was himself both a diabetic, and a lifelong smoker. This looks like hypocrisy, of course, but it might best be understood as a contradiction designed to reveal the inevitable complexities of such issues. As always, he is present in his own poem, and his presence seems to qualify the criticisms he makes, ostensibly undermining both the poem and the poet, and underscoring the point that, to put it simply, life isn't simple! As we saw in *Cosmopolitan Greetings*, Ginsberg's comic poetry is ambivalent, quarrelling with itself in ways that exposes both the complexity of the theme, and humanity of the speaker.

There is ambivalence too in Ginsberg's comic self-deprecation, as we saw in his poem about Fernando Pessoa, where he interrogates his own ego. Often it's informed by his Buddhist inclination to keep the ego in check, but it's important to consider how Ginsberg's readiness to present himself negatively affects the way we perceive persona behind the poems. On occasions he is not unlike a schlemiel, the stock comic character of Jewish folklore: in Lawrence J. Epstein's words, 'A schlemiel (rhymes with reveal) is a pitiful, unlucky, or socially maladjusted person. There is pity toward such a loser'[53]. Though Ginsberg is socially successful in many ways, aspects of his personality align him strongly with this comic type, particularly in old age. We see it in his references to his failing health, for instance, in his sexual inadequacies, and more generally in the struggles he has with his ego. It is evident in his 1985 piece, 'The Guest', collected in *White Shroud*. Here Ginsberg offers a candid admission of his impotence:

> I enter slow, he's soft
> no pain, he raises his behind
> no hard on, hips aloft
> I push, he doesn't mind.
> My trouble is, I'm old
> and tho this young kind boy

---

[53]Lawrence J. Epstein, *The Haunted Smile: The Story of Jewish Comedians in America* (New York: Perseus Books Group, 2001): 302

gives me a chance for joy
I'm not hard enough to be bold.

[*CP*, 919]

Ginsberg presents himself as a rather pathetic figure, and the humour is subtle rather than overt. It resides partly in the image of the flaccid poet's failure, and partly in the tone created by the rhyming short lines: particularly with the pleasing oxymoron soft/aloft. Here Ginsberg has lost his ability to act on desire, and his potential to be desired ('no hard on'); yet it is hard to know if we should admire or pity the speaker's impulse to 'push', and the drive that animates him in the face of his loss and failure.

In the late poem, 'Death and Fame', he imagines his own funeral, viewed as a ceremony where the world pays homage to the famous Beat writer, including acolytes who attest to how the great bard changed their lives. Many of the statements are wonderfully comic, and once more the focus of the irony is often on Ginsberg himself, as with the fan who says: 'I met him dozens of times he never remembered my name I loved/him anyway, true artist'. The poem closes with the lines:

> Deaf & Dumb bards with hand signing quick brilliant gestures
> Then Journalists, editors' secretaries, agents, portraitists & photo-
>   graphy aficionados, rock critics, cultured laborors, cultural
>   historians come to witness the historic funeral
> Super-fans, poetasters, aging Beatniks & Deadheads, autograph-
>   hunters, distinguished paparazzi, intelligent gawkers
> Everyone knew they were part of 'History' except the deceased
> who never knew exactly what was happening even when I was alive

[*CP*, 1132]

Comic images abound here, as they do throughout the poem, but once more it is at the end where Ginsberg delivers the punchline. Despite his fame, he constructs himself as a schlemiel to whom success came despite his bewildered inability to understand the world.

In other poems, such as 'Bowel Song' (1996) he queries his ability to be funny – another example of him questioning his own fame, and the value of his work:

> Allen Ginsberg says, these words'll get you nowhere
> these jokes won't be funny when everyone leaves the seven exits.
>
> [*CP*, 1097]

The poet questions, not just the value of his humour, but his very vocation. This questioning may appear trivial, but it complicates Ginsberg's writing, augmenting the speaker's status as a contradiction, and creating the kind of nuance that critics often deny in his work. Importantly, while the schlemiel is a loser-type character, there can be a degree of dignity in his inadequacy and low status that reinforces our sense of his humanity. Ruth Wisse, for instance, argues that the traditional schlemiel has taken on new forms in contemporary American culture, and the modern schlemiel 'grafted onto his original endowments of weakness, self-control, and capacity to endure'[54]. There is certainly 'capacity to endure' in Ginsberg's persona: it can be seen in the 'push' that motivates the flaccid Ginsberg in 'The Guest', for instance, and most importantly, in the irrepressible humour that ameliorates his failure. While he often lacks the 'self-control' that Wisse also sees in the modern schlemiel, his readiness to laugh at this lack is both entertaining and inspiring.

Conclusion

At the outset it was suggested that Ginsberg's life has tended to eclipse his writing, and doubtless this will continue. His diverse and often flamboyant activities as a Beat, Buddhist, campaigner, polemicist, media personality, pop star, and teacher took the focus off his poetry when he was alive, and perhaps still contribute to some critics' readiness to trivialise his writing. Certainly few poets have divided critics the way Ginsberg has, but hopefully I have helped make a case here for his status as a serious artist. Naturally his writing cannot be detached from the various public roles Ginsberg played, and, as we have seen, his poetry draws heavily on his life, both public and

---

[54]Quoted in Edward Alexander, '*The Dual Image* by Harold Fisch; *The Schlemiel as Modern Hero* by Ruth R. Wisse', *Commentary*, June 1972. Available online https://www.commentarymagazine.com/articles/the-dual-image-by-harold-fisch-the-schlemiel-as-modern-hero-by-ruth-r-wisse/

personal; but it also transcends it. As A. Robert Lee says in a recent book about Beat legacies, 'The notion of his work gathering dust verges on the unlikely'[55], and this is not merely due to his status as a Beat icon. His themes of alienation, grief, guilt, politics, sexual and spiritual longing, and death, are obviously enduring. More importantly, Ginsberg's approach to these themes, informed as it is by a potent comic awareness, helps to keep his work relevant and engaging. Ultimately he can be viewed as a cosmopolitan comic: his humour, with its insistence on ambiguity and nuance, and its resistance to reduction and stasis, seems to offer a vital response to the difficulties we continue to suffer in the modern world.

---

[55] A. Robert Lee, *The Beats: Authorship, Legacies* (Edinburgh: Edinburgh University Press, 2019): 59

SELECTED BIBLIOGRAPHY

IMPORTANT POETRY COLLECTIONS

Howl and Other Poems (1956)

Kaddish and Other Poems (1961)

Empty Mirror: Early Poems (1961)

Reality Sandwiches (1963)

Planet News (1968)

The Gates of Wrath: Rhymed Poems, 1948-1952 (1973)

The Fall of America: Poems of These States (1973)

Iron Horse (1973)

First Blues: Rags, Ballads & Harmonium Songs, 1971-1974 (1975)

Sad Dust Glories: Poems During Work Summer in Woods (1975)

Mind Breaths: Poems 1971-1976 (1978)

Plutonian Ode: Poems 1977-1980 (1981)

Collected Poems 1947-1980 (1984)

White Shroud: Poems 1980-1985 (1986)

Cosmopolitan Greetings: Poems 1986-1992 (1994)

Howl Annotated (1995)

Illuminated Poems (1996)

Selected Poems 1947-1995 (1996)

Death & Fame: Poems 1993-1997 (1999)

Howl & Other Poems: 50th Anniversary Edition (2006)

Collected Poems 1947-1997 (2006)

OTHER NOTABLE WRITING

The Yage Letters (1963) – with William S. Burroughs

Indian Journals: 1970 (1970)

Allen Verbatim: Lectures on Poetry, Politics, Consciousness (1974)

Composed on the Tongue: Literary Conversations 1967-1977 (1980)

Journals Early Fifties Early Sixties (1993)

Journals Mid-Fifties: 1954-1958 (1995)

Deliberate Prose: Selected Essays 1952-1995 (2000)

The Book of Martyrdom and Artifice: First Journals and Poems 1937-1952 (2006)

The Selected Letters of Allen Ginsberg and Gary Snyder (2009)

I Greet You At The Beginning of a Great Career: The Selected Correspondence of Lawrence Ferlinghetti and Allen Ginsberg 1955-1997 (2015)

The Best Minds of My Generation: A Literary History of the Beats (2017)

INTERVIEWS

David Carter (ed), *Allen Ginsberg: Spontaneous Mind, Selected Interviews 1958-1996* (2001)

SELECTED AUDIO RELEASES

The Lion For Real. Produced by Hal Willner, Mouth Almighty/Mercury, 1989, 1996

Cosmopolitan Greetings Jazzy Opera. Music by George Gruntz. Migros-Genossenschafts-Bund, 1993

Hydrogen Jukebox. Music by Philip Glass, libretto by Allen Ginsberg, Elektra Nonesuch, 1993.

Holy Soul Jelly Roll: Poems & Songs 1949-1993. Four CD set, produced by Hal Willner, Rhino Records, 1994

Howl & Other Poems. Fantasy Records, 1998

The Ballad of the Skeletons. With Paul McCartney, Philip Glass, Produced by Lenny Kaye, Mouth Almighty/Mercury, 1996

Wichita Vortex Sutra: Live at St Mark's Church. Produced by Hal Willner; featuring Lenny Kaye, Lee Ranaldo, Steve Shelley, Lenny Pickett, Philip Glass et al. Artemis Records, 2004

The Voice of the Poet. Random House Audio, 2004

The Allen Ginsberg Audio Collection. Harper Audio/Caedmon Collection. 3 CD set, 2004

Songs of Innocence and Experience: William Blake Tuned by Allen Ginsberg. Omnivore Records, 2017

SELECTED SECONDARY SOURCES

Katherine Campbell Mead-Brewer, *The Trickster in Ginsberg: A Critical Reading* by (London: McFarland and Co, 2013)

This book explores the relationship between Ginsberg and the Native American trickster tradition, as manifest in the figure of the Coyote. It focuses principally on 'Howl', and what it sees as the four key elements of the Coyote Trickster: 'Endless appetite [...] a proclivity for creating and falling into tricks and traps [...] boundlessness [...] and transformative power', all of which Mead-Brewer finds in Ginsberg's writing.

Steve Finbow, *Allen Ginsberg* (London: Reaktion Books, 2012)

This book is in the Critical Lives series and presents a succinct account of key stages in Ginsberg's career, together with informed and perceptive readings of essential works. Finbow combines first-hand knowledge of Ginsberg the man, with an understanding of the cultural context in which the writer lived and worked.

Eliot Katz, *The Poetry and Politics of Allen Ginsberg* (Beatdom Books, 2016)

An excellent account of Ginsberg's significance as a political writer – it contains informative chapters on Ginsberg and 60s counterculture, exploring his responses to Vietnam, his relationship with the anti-war movement, antinuclear activism, and so on. He identifies a degree of ideological flexibility in Ginsberg, underpinned by a general optimism and desire for improvement, what the author deems his 'energetic yearnings for healthier human possibilities' [281]

A. Robert Lee, *The Beats: Authorship, Legacies* (Edinburgh: Edinburgh University Press, 2019)

This is one of the most recent general books on the Beat Generation, from an internationally renowned critic. It includes an excellent chapter on Ginsberg, 'Allen Ginsberg: Public Privacy', together with an informed account of the origins of the Beat phenomenon. It also contains sections on the ways in which Beat writing has developed, exploring some of the lesser-known Beat figures, many unjustly neglected by scholarship, including female and African American writers.

Bill Morgan, *I Celebrate Myself: The Somewhat Private Life of Allen Ginsberg* (London: Penguin, 2007)

This is one of the best biographies, written by a distinguished authority on Beat culture. As Ginsberg's archivist and bibliographer, Morgan is able to offer a very useful timeline for the poems alongside his account of the poet's life. He places Ginsberg in a Jewish tradition of industriousness, with an emphasis on his status as a bohemian and a subversive. It's a comprehensive and very readable book.

Jonah Raskin, *American Scream: Allen Ginsberg's 'Howl' and The Making of the Beat Generation* (Berkeley: University of California Press, 2004)

This offers a wide-ranging account of Ginsberg's 'Howl', both in terms of its genesis and its cultural impact. The emphasis is biographical and socio-cultural, but it provides a very useful twenty-first-century perspective on the poem and Ginsberg's early years as a writer.

Michael Schumacher, *Dharma Lion: A Biography of Allen Ginsberg* (Minnesota: University of Minnesota Press, 2016)

The early version of this book appeared in 1992, but at over 800 pages, the expanded edition of Schumacher's biography offers the longest and most detailed account of his life. It is very accessible, however, with a strong narrative drive, and presents a compelling portrait of Ginsberg, together with key figures in the author's life, such as Jack Kerouac, Lucian Carr, and William Burroughs.

Tony Trigilio, *Allen Ginsberg's Buddhist Poetics* (Carbondale: Southern Illinois University Press, 2007)

The author argues that Ginsberg's writing exhibits a 'Buddhist poetics', underpinned by a 'melding' of Eastern and Western philosophies that continues to evolve through the course of his life. While Trigilio's argument is often rather dense and clotted, he demonstrates convincingly how Ginsberg's study of Buddhism and training in Buddhist techniques had a profound influence on his later work.